I0137111

THE PILLARS OF KEDVALE AVENUE:

A GEOGRAPHY OF A CHICAGO WEST SIDE NEIGHBORHOOD IN THE 1960s

Anthony J. Dzik, Ph.D.

SUNFISH BOULEVARD PUBLICATIONS

Portsmouth, Ohio

© *2009* Anthony J. Dzik

The Pillars of Kedvale Avenue: A Geography of a Chicago West Side Neighborhood in the 1960s

ISBN **978-0-578-02727-2**

To the memory of

Mary Falasz, Eva Dzik, and Tina Dzik

ACKNOWDLEGEMENTS

It has been said that it takes a village to raise a child and the completion of this book would not have been possible were it not for a number of people who lived in my old urban village. I would like to thank the following former residents of the neighborhood and environs who provided oral histories, photographs, and sundry information: Linda Adams, Sol Aiello, Stan Camporini, Joseph Choronzak, Ron Ciesla, Ed Cygan, Dolores Firlote, Bob Glowacki, Mike Godzicki, Tim Grzesiakowski, Irene Gwozdz, Ted Idzior, Carolyn Kolssak, Anthony Kurpiewski, Sr. Theresa Lesnak, Ted Lisowski, Greg Lopatka, Peter Lucnik, Lucian Lutek, Winnie Melus, Gladys Pales, Dolores Parzygnat, Dorothy Pawelczak, Roger Plichta, Sharon Quigley, Lillian Rafa, Joe Ripka, Casey Rog, Joseph Salvato, Chet Shafer, Bruce Stachowiak, John Terek, Ron Tragasz, Louise Yankowich, Lou Zajdel, and Patricia Zajdel.

I also extend my thanks to Dr. Mark Bouman of Chicago State University for his photographic contributions and for pointing me in the right direction on some research quests. My heartfelt appreciation is given to Karla Sanders, student at Ohio University, for her outstanding cartography. Special thanks to Connie Salyers Stoner, director of the Clark Memorial Library of Shawnee State University, for helping me access census data, to Joe Piersen of the Chicago & Northwestern Railway Historical Society for photos and information about the 40th St. yard and car shops, to Kathy Maass for the photo of the Andes Candies store #8, to Reggie Ratliff of Community Partners for the Common Good for information on the former Emmaus United Methodist Church, and to Joel Thoreson for the picture and information on Advent Lutheran Church. My appreciation goes out to J. Byrne, Bryan Butler, Micheal Goc, Jerry Kasper, Brian Kuchay, Gordon McAlpin, Marijke Rijsberman, Jay Ruby, Stephen Scalzo, and Joe Testagrose for kindly allowing me to use photos from their collections.

Finally, I must also thank my wife Drema Dzik for her encouragement and for patiently listening to my stories of the old neighborhood.

CONTENTS

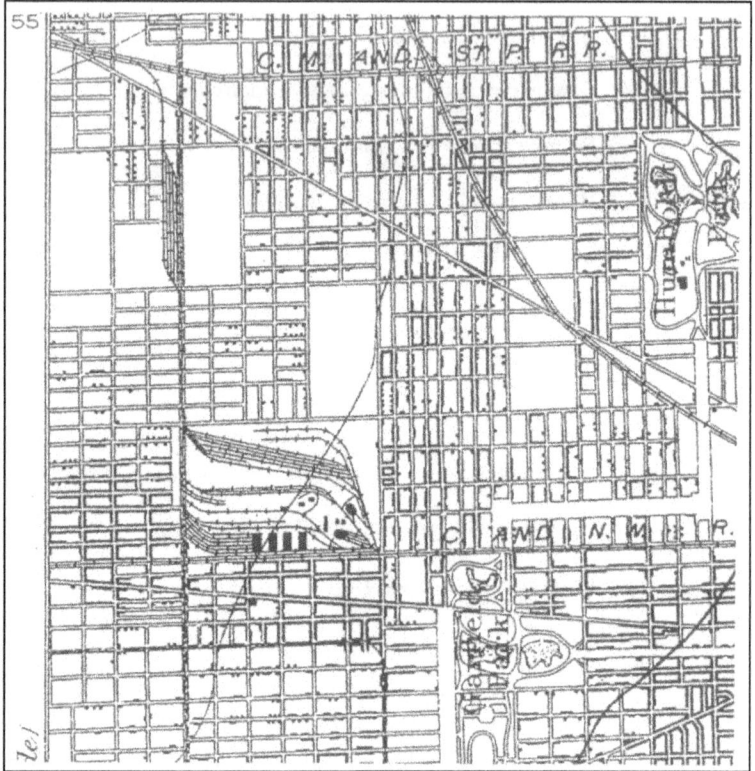

Figure 1. 1901 Topographic map of Chicago's West Side. The neighborhood
of this study is immediately north of the C & NW Railroad 40th St. Yard and
car shops. (Tony Dzik collection).

PROLOGUE:

THE PILLARS OF KEDVALE AVENUE

The physical pillars of Kedvale Avenue are concrete subdivision markers erected in the early 20th Century at some intersections in my old West Side neighborhood in Chicago. Some of these pillars still stand in 2009, a testament to their solid sturdy construction.

Figure 2. Pillars at Kedvale Avenue and Thomas St. (Photo by Mark Bouman)

The spiritual pillars of Kedvale Avenue are the people who resided in the neighborhood during the 1960s. They were also of solid sturdy construction. They were largely a working class people with strong ethics who worked, worshipped, and recreated with determination. They married each other and buried each other and in between passed onto to their children values such as honest work, love of God, and love of country. Almost a half of a century has passed and today those sturdy pillars who remain in this world are scattered from Posen to Palatine. Yet, the sense of neighborhood carries on as friendships cultivated on the West Side have withstood the years and the miles.

Figure 3. Multi-unit apartment building in the 1100 block of N. Kildare (Photo by Mark Bouman).

CHAPTER 1:

INTRODUCTION

My mom was a funeral junkie. That was my impression while growing up on Chicago's West Side in the 1950s and 1960s. It seemed that just about every week until I reached the age of 12 or 13 she would drag me along with her to one of the local funeral parlors where she paid her respects to a dearly departed neighbor. Sometimes as we knelt by the casket to say a silent "Eternal Rest" or "Ave Maria", I'd find myself wondering why we were there. In my young mind, the deceased was just some old lady with a basset hound who used to live across from Noga's or some Joe Schmoe from Iowa Street who used to wear funny horn-rimmed glasses. The departed were probably faint acquaintances, but we really didn't know them all that well.

As I grew in years and wisdom, I came to realize that there were quite a few regular callers at many of these wakes. They were neighbors, fellow parishioners, and business folk who seemed to share some common bond. They were the same souls I saw at Sunday Mass, the same folks who waited each weekday morning for the #70 Division Street bus, the same people shopping at the little corner grocery on Saturday afternoon. I sort of knew their names and a lot of them seemed to know mine. So many times I heard someone yell

"Anthony, if you don't stop bouncing that ball against my garage, I'm gonna call up your matka!"

or

"Antek, I better not catch ya smoking cigarettes in my gangway again!"

Sometimes the admonishments were in English, other times in Polish or Slovak, and on an occasion or two in some invented on-the-spot hybrid English and East European tongue. A random correction might also be delivered with an Italian accent. Lest the reader conclude that I was notorious punk, I also was lauded at times with

"Antosz, you such a dobry boyshik for helping your matka like dat."

(Note: Although there were very few Jewish residents of the

neighborhood, many older Polish-speakers used a few quasi-Yiddish words such as "boyshik" and "ustemp". These terms may have been picked up in the old country or from Jewish shopkeepers in the Madison-Pulaski shopping area a mile south of the neighborhood). What amazed me was that incidents like these not only occurred two or three doors down from my home, but also three or four blocks away. This was truly an urban village.

Renowned Chicago newspaper columnist Mike Royko once described such urban villages as "neighborhood-towns" where one would find all of the elements and institutions of the small town—the local tavern, the corner grocery, the funeral home, the neighborhood sports star, the neighborhood club, the neighborhood drunk, the neighborhood politician, the church, the main street (Royko: 1971). The majority of the residents of such a neighborhood-town are of the same ethnicity and a strong sense of community exists. Royko could have been writing about my neighborhood in the 1960s as it possessed most of the traits he described.

The 1960s were a turbulent decade for the nation and for Chicago. Attitudes were changing, values were being adjusted, and demographics were shifting. Central city populations were declining and the suburbs were expanding. Where and how we worked, shopped, and played was changing.

In our urban village, there was something in the air, but we barely noticed it, or maybe we opted to ignore it for at least a little while. Nearby areas such as West Garfield Park and Austin had or were beginning to experience demographic change, but our little corner of the West Side (or was it the Northwest Side? This will be addressed in a later chapter) seemed to have stability. Culturally and economically our little urban village had not changed much since the 1940s and as the 1960s dawned, it appeared that continued stability and tranquility were assured. Surprisingly, the neighborhood was left temporarily unscathed by the Humboldt Park riot of 1966 and the devastation of North Lawndale following the assassination of Dr. Martin Luther King, Jr. in 1968.

The 1970s brought about the true onset of change. An era was ending. The older residents were dying off and their children were beginning to leave the area for the greener lawns of suburban Norridge and Niles.

This book presents a picture in time of the geography of what might lovingly be called the last urban village on Chicago's West Side. This is an examination of the geography, social history, and economy of a small corner of the 31st Ward during the 1960s.

Figure 4. Bungalows at Iowa St. and Kolin Ave (Tony Dzik Collection).

CHAPTER 2:

GEOGRAPHY, BOUNDARIES, AND TOPONYMS

In the 1920s, Ernest W. Burgess and other sociologists from the University of Chicago divided the city into 75 community areas (In 1960, two additional community areas were added to bring the total to 77). The Chicago School of Sociology contended that cities were comprised of "natural areas" whose general character and socioeconomic composition remained stable over time even as their ethnic/racial make-ups changed (Seligman: 2005). The boundaries of the community areas were originally based upon a number of considerations such as the settlement history of the area, local identification with the area, the local trade area, and natural and man-made barriers such as railroad tracks, branches of the Chicago River, and city parks. Today, the 77 Community Areas (Figure 5) are mainly utilized as geo-statistical units for analyzing various economic and demographic data.

The neighborhood as defined in this study is located in Community Area 23 Humboldt Park. While many neighborhood residents occasionally visited the 207-acre park from which the community area derives its name, few would identify Humboldt Park as being the name of their area (It is interesting to note that most of the park's acreage lies outside of the Humboldt Park Community Area's eastern boundary).

Specifically the boundaries of the neighborhood in this study are Pulaski Road on the east, Chicago Avenue on the south, the Belt Line Railway on the west, and North Avenue on the north. Figure 6 depicts the neighborhood's land use patterns in the 1960s. The Chicago and Northwestern railway yard just south of Chicago Avenue clearly separated the neighborhood from the West Garfield Park community area. The Belt Line railroad tracks (Figure 7) and the corridor of industry west of Kostner Avenue isolated the neighborhood from the Austin community. On the north and east, the largely commercial North Avenue and Pulaski Road thoroughfares served to delineate a separation of neighborhoods. There on the north and east, the demarcation was somewhat permeable because many residents of the neighborhood would occasionally venture outward for a few city blocks while shopping or socializing.

Chicago's 77 Community Areas

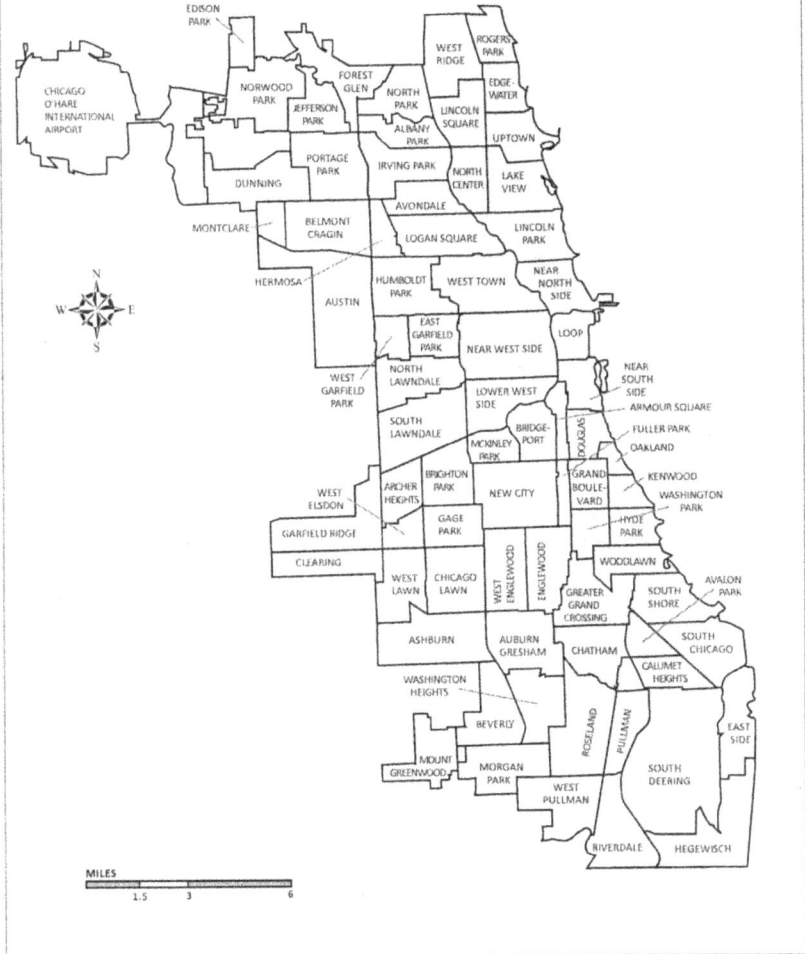

EDISON PARK

WEST RIDGE

ROGERS PARK

CHICAGO O'HARE INTERNATIONAL AIRPORT

FOREST GLEN

NORWOOD PARK

EDGE-WATER

NORTH PARK

LINCOLN SQUARE

JEFFERSON PARK

ALBANY PARK

UPTOWN

PORTAGE PARK

IRVING PARK

NORTH CENTER

LAKE VIEW

DUNNING

AVONDALE

MONTCLARE

BELMONT CRAGIN

LINCOLN PARK

LOGAN SQUARE

HERMOSA

HUMBOLDT PARK

WEST TOWN

NEAR NORTH SIDE

AUSTIN

EAST GARFIELD PARK

NEAR WEST SIDE

LOOP

WEST GARFIELD PARK

NORTH LAWNDALE

NEAR SOUTH SIDE

LOWER WEST SIDE

ARMOUR SQUARE

SOUTH LAWNDALE

BRIDGE-PORT

DOUGLAS

FULLER PARK

MCKINLEY PARK

OAKLAND

WEST ELSDON

ARCHER HEIGHTS

BRIGHTON PARK

NEW CITY

GRAND BOULE-VARD

KENWOOD

WASHINGTON PARK

GARFIELD RIDGE

GAGE PARK

HYDE PARK

CLEARING

WEST ENGLEWOOD

ENGLEWOOD

WOODLAWN

WEST LAWN

CHICAGO LAWN

GREATER GRAND CROSSING

SOUTH SHORE

AVALON PARK

ASHBURN

AUBURN GRESHAM

CHATHAM

SOUTH CHICAGO

WASHINGTON HEIGHTS

CALUMET HEIGHTS

BEVERLY

ROSELAND

PULLMAN

EAST SIDE

MOUNT GREENWOOD

MORGAN PARK

SOUTH DEERING

WEST PULLMAN

RIVERDALE

HEGEWISCH

W N E S

MILES
1.5   3   6

Figure 5. Chicago Community Areas (Cartography by Karla Sanders)

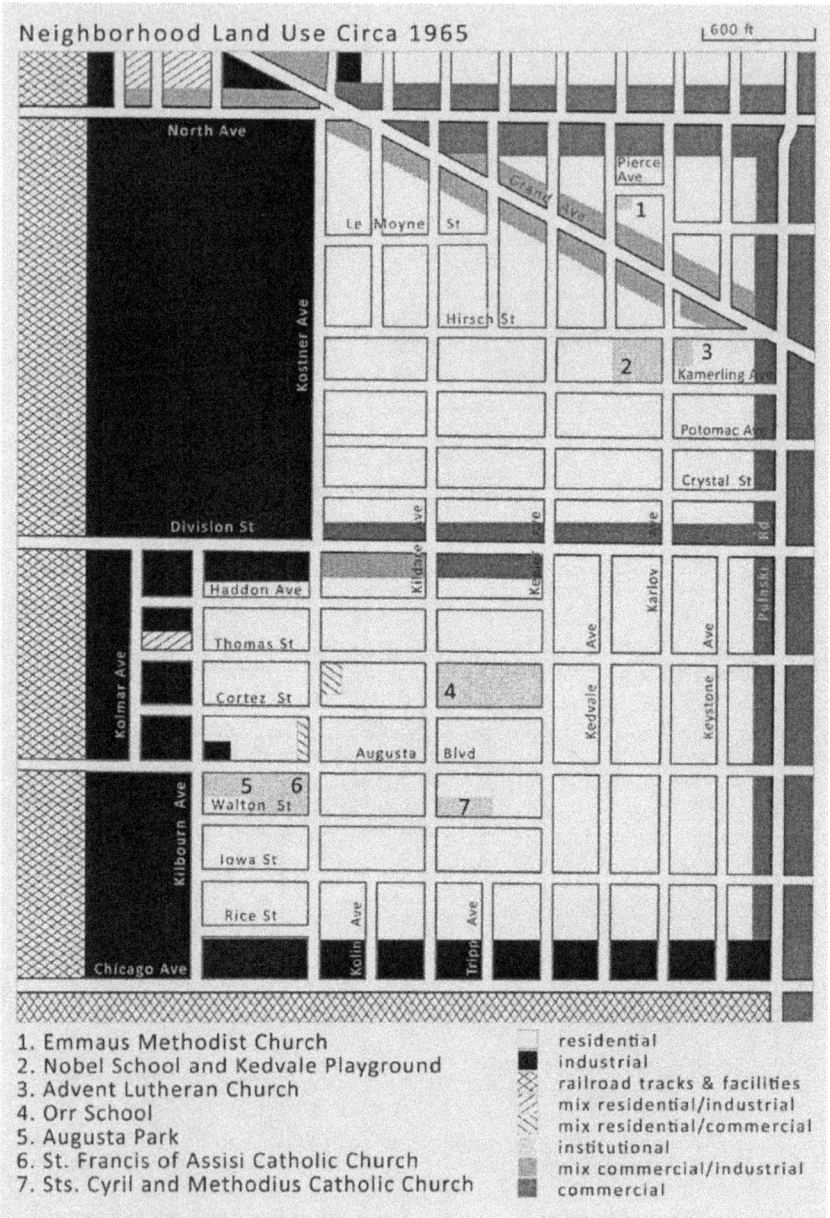

Neighborhood Land Use Circa 1965 | 600 ft

North Ave
Pierce Ave
Le Moyne St
Grand Ave
Kostner Ave
Hirsch St
1
2
3
Kamerling Ave
Potomac Ave
Crystal St
Division St
Kildare Ave
Keeler Ave
Karlov Ave
Pulaski Rd
Haddon Ave
Thomas St
Kolmar Ave
Cortez St
Kedvale Ave
Keystone Ave
4
Augusta Blvd
5 6
Walton St
Kilbourn Ave
7
Iowa St
Rice St
Kolin Ave
Tripp Ave
Chicago Ave

1. Emmaus Methodist Church
2. Nobel School and Kedvale Playground
3. Advent Lutheran Church
4. Orr School
5. Augusta Park
6. St. Francis of Assisi Catholic Church
7. Sts. Cyril and Methodius Catholic Church

residential
industrial
railroad tracks & facilities
mix residential/industrial
mix residential/commercial
institutional
mix commercial/industrial
commercial

Figure 6. Neighborhood Land Use (Cartography by Karla Sanders).

Figure 7. Belt Line viaduct over Division Street in 2009 (Photo by Mark Bouman).

In terms of 1970 census tracts, the area falls entirely within tracts 2306 and 2313 (Figure 8). In the 1960 Census the tracts were numbered 277 and 278. Politically, the neighborhood is located within Chicago's 31st Ward.

The neighborhood was located approximately seven miles west-northwest of the Loop. Travel to the downtown by automobile was generally done by taking Augusta Boulevard east to Milwaukee Ave or the Kennedy Expressway either of which would bring the commuter or shopper to the Loop. An alternate route was Augusta Blvd. east to Hamlin (Independence Blvd), then southward through West Garfield Park where one could enter onto the Congress (Eisenhower) Expressway for the journey to downtown.

The main public transit route to the Loop was the #70 Division Street C.T.A. bus route which during the early 1960s began at Division Street and Austin Blvd. (6000 W.) and ended near the intersection of Wabash Ave and Van Buren St. at the south end of the Loop. For a faster journey one could take the Division bus to the old Polish "downtown" at Division and Ashland and take the Milwaukee-Dearborn subway line to the Loop. Some neighborhood people, particularly those who lived at the southeastern edge, would utilize the C.T.A.'s Lake Street Elevated line entering at 300 N. Pulaski Rd which was approximately five or six city blocks distant.

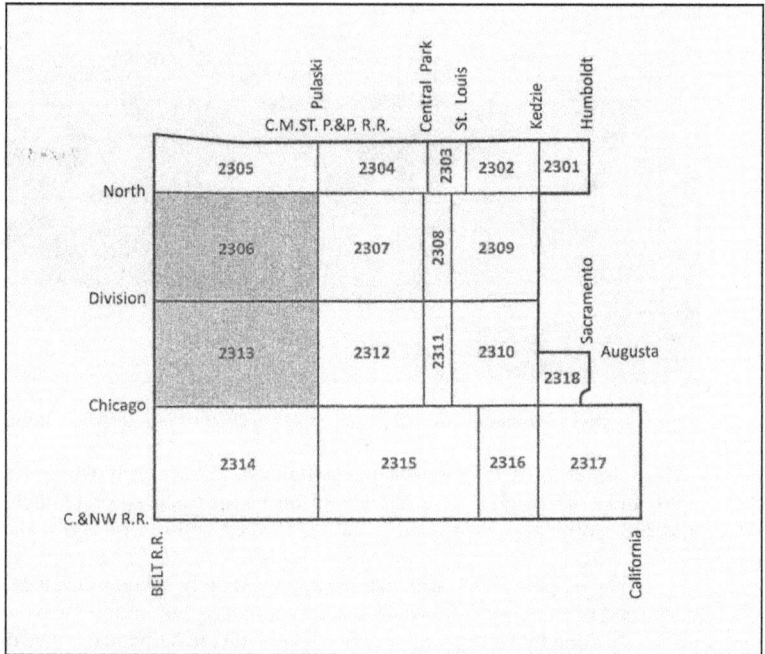

Figure 8. Census tracts in Humboldt Park Community Area (Cartography by Karla Sanders).

Toponyms or place names can sometimes provide insight into an area's settlement date and early history, the national origins or early settlers, local economic activities, or important figures from the community's formative years. Up to this point, the study area has been referred to as "the neighborhood" or "our urban village" and no definitive toponym has been provided. The provision of a definitive toponym is not to be. In fact, there is some discretion as to whether or not the neighborhood is even on the West Side!

Many people who resided in the area during the 1950s and 1960s often referred to their neighborhood as being on Chicago's West Side, but some would contend that they were located on the Northwest Side. An informal survey of former residents shows that 69% identified themselves as West Siders, 26% perceived the neighborhood to be on the Northwest Side, and 5% said they used both regional markers. When pressed further for a neighborhood name, 57% of the respondents could not think of anything definite. This is not surprising for a neighborhood located on the periphery of an "official" community area. Rev. Lowell Streiker writes about growing up in the 1940s at 635 N. Springfield "in a neighborhood with no distinct name but variably described by observers as 'West Garfield Park', 'West Chicago', and 'Humboldt Park.' "(Streiker:2006).

Table 1 shows the breakdown of the neighborhood name survey. 23% called the neighborhood "Francziskowo", a Chicago Polish-American Roman Catholic toponym referring to St. Francis of Assisi Church located at Kostner Ave. and Augusta Blvd. Polish immigrants in Chicago often identified with the parish environs and vernacular regions like "Trojcowo" (Holy Trinity parish) and "Jadwigowo" (St. Hedwig's) were generally well known in Polish-American communities. A few respondents (11%) related that the neighborhood was sometimes referred to as "The Patch", a term going back to around 1910 when parts of the neighborhood were still semi-rural and pumpkin and other vegetable patches were part of local land use. (In Chicago, the term "The Patch" is occasionally applied as a local identifier in other neighborhoods as well, particularly in reference to the old Italian-American immigrant neighborhood in the vicinity of Grand Avenue and Western Avenue). A mere handful of respondents identified the neighborhood as "West Humboldt Park" and the hybrid "Northwest Town" was mentioned once.

It seems that in the 21st Century, the neighborhood finally acquired an agreed-upon vernacular topynym. Many current residents call the area "K-town", a reference to the succession of north-south street names that begin with the letter "K" (Keystone, Kedvale, Kildare, etc.). The history of these street names goes back to a city plan adopted in 1913 to name Chicago's streets in alphabetic order from the Indiana border going west. The plan was not fully implemented except for west of Crawford Ave/Pulaski Road (4000 W.) an area that had been recently annexed into the city and was still relatively sparsely settled. "K" is the eleventh letter in the alphabet and that indicates that the K-town streets are eleven miles east of the Indiana border.

Table 1. Names for the Neighborhood

Response   %

Response	%
No name	57
Francziskowo	23
The "Patch"	11
West Humboldt Park	8
Northwest Town	1

After Cicero Ave. (4800 W.), north-south streets begin with the letter "L" (e.g., Lamon, Latrobe, Long) and past Central Ave. (5600 W.), north-south streets begin with the letter "M" (e.g., Major, Menard, Monitor). "N", "O", and "P" streets follow up to the city's western limits.

CHAPTER 3:

DEMOGRAPHICS AND ETHNICITY

The population of the neighborhood during the 1960s hovered about the 14,000 mark. If the neighborhood had been its own political entity, that figure would easily place it into a "small city" classification.

The 1960 United States Census tallied 13,824 people in the two census tracts that comprised the neighborhood and the 1970 Census showed the population to be 14,294 (Table 2). Both tracts had similar numbers in 1960, but by 1970, the northern tract (277/2306) had grown by 1295 persons, and the southern tract (278/2313) had lost 825.These changes likely occurred for several reasons:

1. There were more 5+ unit apartment buildings and more rental units in general in the northern tract.
2. The population of the northern tract grew as there was an influx of white people fleeing demographic changes in the Humboldt Park neighborhoods to the east.
3. There was an exodus of families from the southern tract that may have been in part a response to the Our Lady of the Angels School fire of 1958 (See Chapter 9). Some of these families were large and the new owners of their properties tended to be smaller families (Source: oral histories).

In terms of age structure, the population was a somewhat mature one. Median age was about 35 (1970 Census). Children 0-13 years of age accounted for about 13% of the population. 11% of residents were 65+ years old, a figure slightly above the percentage for all of Chicago.

The traditional nuclear family was the neighborhood's most typical household. Over 90% of children under the age of 18 lived with both parents. Fewer than 13% of families were headed by a female.

The neighborhood's population was largely comprised of working-class and middle-income people. 1970 median family income was $10,265 for census tract 2306 and $10,709 for tract 2313. Both figures were just a little above the median for all of Chicago ($10,242). Almost one-half of employed residents worked in the manufacturing sector. Only about 12%

worked in a white collar classification. It is not surprising that, with the large number of industrial and commercial ventures within the area, 17.5% of workers reported that they walked to work.

Typical of a largely blue collar population with about 20% of residents being foreign-born, the median number of school years completed (roughly 9.5 years) was less than that for Chicago as a whole (11.2). Only about 28.5% or neighborhood residents over 25 years of age had graduated high school; a little less than 3% possessed a college degree.

If home and automobile ownership are any indication, a goodly number of residents were participating in the "American Dream". Home ownership in the southern tract was way above the Chicago norm with 49% of housing units being owner-occupied. For the northern tract, the figure was 31.4%, but it must be kept in mind, that there were many more multi-unit properties there. About 70% of households in the neighborhood owned at least one automobile.

During the decade, the neighborhood's population was almost entirely white and of European ancestry. Approximately 20% of the population had been born overseas. The Census classified more than one-half of the neighborhood's population as being of foreign stock. This designation is applied to foreign-born persons and natives of foreign or mixed parentage. Table 3 shows the neighborhood breakdown in numbers of persons of foreign stock. Poland was the dominant source of foreign stock accounting for around one-quarter of it in the northern tract (277/2306) and over one-third in the southern tract (278/2313). Italy ranked second. Czechoslovakia and Germany were third and fourth respectively. Austria, Hungary, and the former Soviet Union when combined accounted for 7% of the neighborhood's foreign stock.

Some problems arise from the Census designations when describing ancestries. One possible conflict is Czechoslovakia, a political entity where several separate ethnicities (Czech, Slovak, Moravian, and Bohemian) can be recognized. While there are cultural, linguistic, and historic ties between these groups, each group tends to distinguish itself. Other mis-classifications might have arisen from the former Austro- Hungarian Empire and the partition of Poland prior to the First World War. Polish territory had been claimed by Austria, Russia, and Prussia (Germany) and those countries would have been named on immigrants' entry papers.

TABLE 2 . NEIGHBORHOOD POPULATION BY CENSUS TRACT* 1960 & 1970

	1960		1970	
Census tract	277	278	2306	2313
Total Population	6804	7020	8099	6195
White	6773	7015	8002	6172
Black	0	0	10	1
Other	31	5	87	22
% White	99.5	99.9	98.8	99.6
% Black	0	0	0.1	0.01
% Other	0.5	0.1	1.1	0.4

*   Census tract numbering changed in 1970 Census, but the tract boundaries remained the same.

TABLE 3. FOREIGN STOCK POPULATION

	1960		1970	
Census Tract	*277*	*278*	*2306*	*2313*
Total Population	6804	7020	8099	6195
Foreign Stock	3312	3938	3781	3605
United Kingdom	111	124	104	62
Ireland	104	86	131	111
Norway	135	67	not reported	
Sweden	69	43	36	12
Germany	398	248	274	177
Poland	763	1346	996	1389
Czechoslovakia	205	501	177	239
Austria	106	82	144	27
Hungary	75	24	52	22
U.S.S.R.	144	93	132	106
Italy	873	1006	895	1070
Other	329	318	840	390

To present another picture of the ethnic composition of the neighborhood, the author performed an analysis of surnames from the 1962 Chicago telephone directory. Surname analysis is a valid method of estimating a population's ethnic make-up (Bramadat and Seljak, 2008; Lauderdale and Kestenbaum, 2000). Table 4 presents the general estimates of the neighborhood's ancestral composition. The reader must be mindful that there may be some misclassification due to intermarriage and the Anglicization of surnames by some persons. However, it is believed that this is a very minor problem as the results of this analysis are similar to Census findings regarding foreign stock.

TABLE 4. Estimates of Ancestry Composition From Surname Analysis

Census Tract	277 (2306)	278 (2313)	Neighborhood Total
Ancestry	*%*	*%*	*%*
Eastern European*	28.3	46.0	38.4
Italian	16.3	21.0	19.1
Anglo-Irish**	22.5	15.9	18.8
German	16.6	9.4	12.5
Scandinavian***	9.7	4.4	6.6
Other/Undetermined	6.8	3.2	4.6

*Polish, Slovak, Czech, Ukrainian, Russian, and Lithuanian

**English, Irish, and Scottish

***Swedish, Norwegian, and Danish

Just like in the Census data, the majority group was Eastern European accounting for 38.4% of the population. The southern census tract was 46% Eastern European. Poles were the largest Slavic subgroup and accounted for a little more than 2/3 of the neighborhood's Eastern European ancestry. Slovaks comprised the bulk of the rest of persons with Slavic ancestry. A mere handful of Czechs, Lithuanians, and other Eastern Europeans resided in the area.

People with Italian ancestry accounted for a little over 19% of the population, followed by the Anglo-Irish group (English, Irish, and Scottish surnames) with 18.8%. German ancestry (12.5%) was well-represented especially in the northern tract. There was a small Scandinavian (largely Swedish and Norwegian) representation that was most evident in the northern tract. It is interesting to note that in 1920 Swedes were the single largest ethnic group in the neighborhood, but their numbers began to fall off as immigration from Sweden dwindled after 1920 (Olson, 1995). Most newcomers to the neighborhood after 1920 were of Polish and Italian descent.

A street-by-street analysis of surname occurrence found several notable geographic clusterings (Figure 9).

1. The vast majority of people with Swedish and Norwegian ancestries lived north of Division Street with a distinct cluster existing in the vicinity of Karlov Avenue and Hirsch Street.
2. Although Polish-Americans were found throughout the neighborhood, the most apparent cluster was in the area bounded by Haddon on the north, Kildare on the east, Walton on the south, and Kilbourn on the west. Smaller clusters existed near Iowa and Kostner and Crystal and Kostner.
3. Italian ancestry was also found throughout the neighborhood, but was especially concentrated in the southern tract east of Keeler Avenue. A large cluster existed in the area of Karlov and Iowa and a smaller, but distinct cluster was found in the vicinity of Division and Karlov.
4. A majority of Slovaks lived in the vicinity of Sts. Cyril and Methodius Catholic Church on Kildare north of Walton. Their most distinct cluster was found in the area bounded by Thomas on the north, Kedvale on the east, Iowa on the south and Kildare on the west.

5. Anglo-Irish and German surnames were found throughout the study area, but were most prevalent in the northern tract. These groups, however, tended to be more dispersed than the other nationalities and did not exhibit any remarkable clusters.

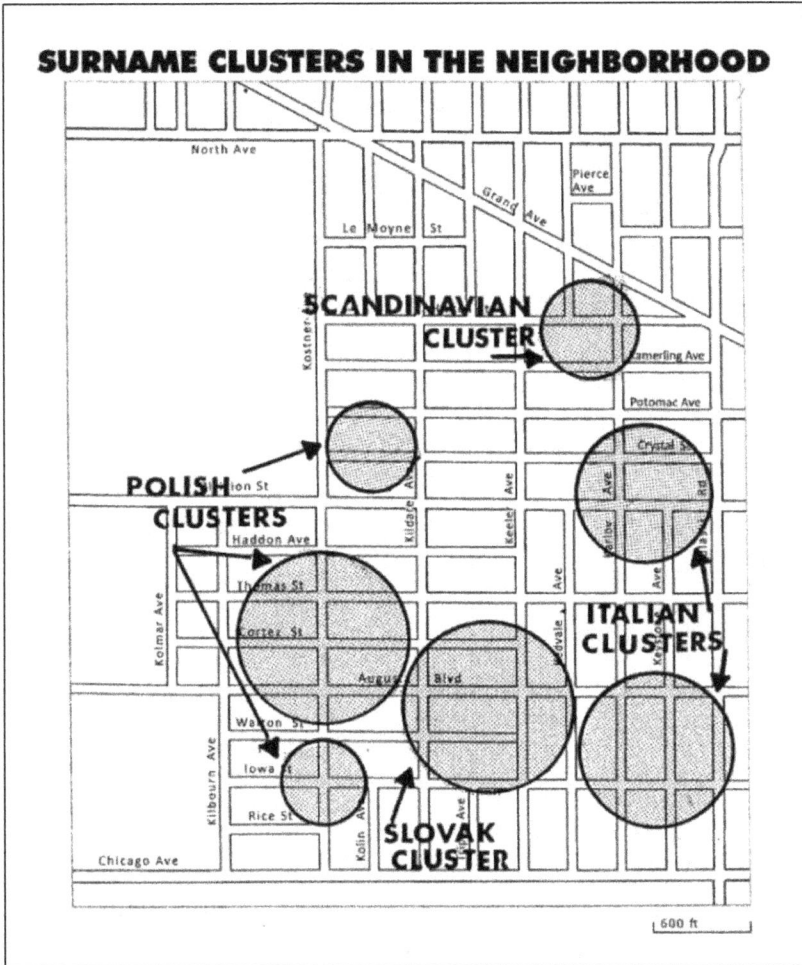

SURNAME CLUSTERS IN THE NEIGHBORHOOD

Figure 9. Major ethnic clusters (Cartography by Karla Sanders and T. Dzik).

Relations between the various ethnic groups were generally quite good. Most people interacted at church, in the local marketplaces, in the workplace, and at recreational venues. Intermarriage was fairly commonplace, especially between Catholics of different ancestries. The majority of residents were second or third generation and for most the old notions of separation between and distrust of other European nationalities had largely faded away. Vestiges of prior separation behavior sometimes arose when people referred to St. Francis as "the Polish Church" or Our Lady of the Angels" as "the Italian parish", but the 1960s reality was that all the churches and parochial schools had some parishioners who were not of the founding ethnic group's background. This is not to say that derogatory terms like "Polack", "Dago", "Mick", or "Herring-choker" were never uttered in the neighborhood. These words were still part of Chicago's working-class lexicon, but were usually reserved for private conversation and not yelled out loud across the alley. It was more likely that epithets would be directed at outsiders, especially Hispanics and African-Americans.

In the 1960s, minorities were conspicuous by their absence from the neighborhood. Residents, however, kept a wary eye focused on adjacent neighborhoods that were in the throes of demographic change. To the east, Humboldt Park was growing increasingly Puerto Rican and West Garfield Park to the south was experiencing a rapid shift from 81% White in 1960 to 97% Black in 1970. To the west, Austin was changing slowly, but by 1980, that community area would be almost three-quarters Black.

During the decade of the 60s, a few African-Americans and Hispanics moved into the neighborhood (Table 5). While their arrival may not have been met with enthusiasm, neither they greeted with overt animosity. As the number of minority residents gradually increased during the 1970s, the White population began a slow, but steady exodus. Demographic change accelerated as the 1980s progressed and by the end of the Century the neighborhood's White population had fallen to 18%. The neighborhood's demographic transformation was much slower than that of West Garfield Park which radically changed within 10 years and Austin's transition which took 20 years (See Table 6). Factors that may account for the neighborhood's slower rate of change are:

1. The population's attachment to the neighborhood Catholic churches. Many residents were hesitant to leave the close-knit community anchored by St. Francis and Sts. Cyril and Methodius parishes. In fact, a number of former residents who had moved to

Galewood, Norwood Park and the near suburbs continued to periodically attend Mass and church recreational functions as late as 1990 (Source: oral histories).

2. Many homeowners had resided in their homes for 20+ years and their mortgages had been paid off. There would have been some reluctance to assume the new financial responsibilities associated with relocation.

3. The physical plant of the neighborhood was newer than that of most of the Humboldt Park area and the adjacent community areas of Austin and West Garfield Park. By the 1960s, those areas had a considerable amount of housing stock deteriorated by age and undermaintenance while the neighborhood's housing stock was still quite sound.

4. The neighborhood's geography may have partially contributed to its longer stability by isolating it from adjacent communities. The Chicago & Northwestern yard south of Chicago was a physical barrier separating the neighborhood from West Garfield Park and the Belt Line tracks and adjacent industries served as a buffer from Austin. The commercial strips of North Avenue and Pulaski Road may have also contributed to the isolation effect.

TABLE 5. NEIGHBORHOOD POPULATION* 1960-2000

	1960	1970	1980	1990	2000
Total Population	13,824	14,294	13,738	16,040	15,202
White	13,788	14,294	8,725	4,014	2,735
Black	0	11	552	8,262	8,940
Other	36	109	4,461	3,764	3,527
% White	99.7	99.2	63.5	25.0	18.0
% Black	0.0	0.1	4.0	51.5	58.9
% Other	0.3	0.7	32.5	23.5	23.2
* Two census tracts combined.					

TABLE 6. RACIAL COMPOSITION OF ADJACENT
COMMUNITY AREAS 1960-1980

	1960	1970	1980
WEST GARFIELD PARK			
% White	83.65	2.82	0.73
% Black	15.79	96.83	98.85
AUSTIN			
% White	99.83	66.35	20.77
% Black	0.02	32.49	73.78

CHAPTER 4:

HOUSING

The neighborhood was part of rural unincorporated Cook County, but was annexed by the city of Chicago in 1889. By the turn of the century, the area was still sparsely populated. The few people living in the area had been attracted to it because of the Chicago & Northwestern Railway's facilities and shops near Chicago Avenue. These facilities and the north-south trackage of the Belt Line Railway around 4600 W. were also beginning to attract industries both large and small. This in turn generated an influx of workers into the area which had a considerable amount of vacant land for building.

Subdivision tends to occur in advance of the need for urban lots (Monchow, 1939). The West Chicago Land Company and several developers such as Frank J. Wisner obtained land in the area and subdivisions were laid out. Wisner, a Chicago businessman with interests in mining, soft drinks (He is credited with inventing the "black cow" or root beer float), and real estate, envisioned an exclusive gated community in the area for upper middle class people of Irish extraction. The "pillars" of Kedvale Avenue addressed in this book's prologue mark what was the probable location for this development. The gated community never materialized, but some of the concrete stanchions remain standing in 2009. What did materialize in the neighborhood was the development of modest homes and apartment buildings affordable to the working and middle classes.

By the late 1920s, the neighborhood was definitely part of the 'bungalow belt". Most bungalows were rectangular brick structures with a modestly pitched, hip-raftered roof and a small front porch. This type of house was ideal for long narrow city lots that generally were 25 to 37 feet wide and 125 feet deep. The typical Chicago Bungalow was a one and one-half story single family home with a full basement. Floor plans were similar to those of earlier one-story working-class homes. On some streets, for example the 800 block of North Kolin (Figure 10), there would be a number of Chicago Bungalows side- by-side. Although the general form of each house was similar, most would have a distinguishing feature or two.

Most of the homes and apartment buildings standing in the neighborhood in the 1960s were built between 1920 and World War II.

According to the 1970 U.S. Census almost 90% of the housing units had been constructed prior to 1939. Median value of housing units north of Division St. was $17,400 and south of Division the median was $18,500. For comparison, the median value for all of Chicago was $21,200. The vast majority of residences were of brick construction. There were single-family bungalows, 2 and 3 flat buildings, and 2 and 3-story multi-unit apartment buildings. Many of the apartment buildings were located on corner lots. In the late 1950s and early 1960s, some of the older wood frame homes built before 1920 were demolished and in their place were constructed single-family brick ranch style homes.

The most common residential building in the neighborhood was the 2-flat. Almost 51% of housing units in the southern census tract and 40% in the northern tract were of this type. 3-flat buildings (Figures 11 & 12) were also conspicuous, especially on Thomas St. and Augusta Blvd. There were more single-family homes south of Division and more 5+ unit apartment buildings (Figures 13 & 14) in the northern tract where one-quarter of the housing units were of this category.

While apartment buildings could be found on most blocks, there were none on Kedvale, Karlov, and Keystone Avenues north of Augusta and south of Division. This area corresponds to the Pillars of Kedvale section that was originally envisioned by the developer to become an exclusive gated community. Almost all of the structures here are single-family homes.

Most housing units were heated with natural gas or electricity. There were, however, still a few buildings that had coal-fired furnaces. The coal chute (Figure 15) identified those that were using or had used that fuel at one time. Many of those buildings were serviced by the Chicago Wood and Coal Co. whose yard was at 4500 W. Chicago Avenue.

Figure 10. Hexagon-style single-family bungalows on the 800 block of N. Kolin Ave. (Photo by Mark Bouman).

Figure 11. 3-flat brick building at 4307 W. Thomas (T. Dzik collection).

Figure 12. 3-flat brick building at 4252 W. Cortez (Photo courtesy of I. Gwozdz).

Figure 13. Multi-unit apartment building at Walton and Keeler (T. Dzik collection).

Figure 14. Multi-unit apartment building at 4059 W. Hirsch (T.Dzik collection).

Figure 15. Typical coal chute door (Photo by Bryan Butler, B2 Graphic Design).

CHAPTER 5:

INDUSTRIAL ACTIVITIES

There was a vast expanse of vacant land on the West Side in the 1870s. The Chicago and Northwestern Railway obtained a large parcel in the vicinity of Kinzie Street and 40th Street and developed their 40th St. Yard (Figure 16). These facilities eventually were bounded on the north by Chicago Avenue, on the east by 40th St. (later renamed Crawford Avenue, then Pulaski Rd.), on the south by the railroad's main line, and on the west (near Kilpatrick Ave.) by the Belt Line Railway.

Figure 16. C&NW 40th St. Yard circa 1955. In the foreground are diesel locomotive servicing facilities near Kinzie St. The marshalling yard near Chicago Ave. is at the top of the picture. (Photo courtesy of Joseph Piersen, C&NW Historical Society Archives).

The freight marshalling yard was situated near Chicago Avenue. Between the yard and the main line tracks were locomotive facilities and a large shop complex. The shops and other railroad facilities were catalysts for population growth in the area. The C&NW and the nearby Belt Railway in combination with land availability attracted a number of industries to the neighborhood. Intersection of a belt line and a trunk line was often a factor in the development of Chicago's manufacturing districts (Monchow, 1939).

In the decades following the Second World War, the shops were closed and demolished and some of the land was sold to industrial concerns. By the late 1960s the 40th St. yard had become obsolete and some of the activities were shifted to the newer Proviso Yard in the western suburbs. In 1980 the yard was embargoed by the government and could no longer be utilized. The diesel locomotive facilities near Kinzie St, however, as of 2009, are still in operation servicing the Metra commuter locomotives. The Belt Line (a transfer carrier) still operates on the north-south trackage near Kolmar Ave.

The industries that located near the railroads varied in size from small machine shops to complexes that occupied an entire city block or more. Although some factories, especially those constructed in the earlier days, were multi-story buildings, many single-story plants were developed in this West Side industrial zone. After the 1920s, operations in many industries had changed to assembly line production and it was more efficient to have all phases of manufacturing located on one level. The relatively large amount of available land in and about the neighborhood was conducive for siting such plants. Another locational advantage for industries on the West Side lay in the fact that traffic congestion in this area was far less than in the older established industrial zones closer to the city center

In the 1960s, the north side of Chicago Avenue along the C&NW yard limits was home to a number of small and medium-sized shops manufacturing machine tools and similar products. Endure Tool and Engineering, F & B Manufacturing, Simplomatic Metal Stampings, and Simonsen Metal Industries all were operating on Chicago Avenue during the 1960s. Food processing was also part of this area's landscape. The Hawthorn Melody Dairy plant and distribution center was located at Chicago Ave. and Tripp St. The building is still used today by Becker Dairy Products. Burney Brothers Bakeries (Schlosser's) was at 4600 W. Chicago Avenue near Kilpatrick just west of the Belt Railway tracks.

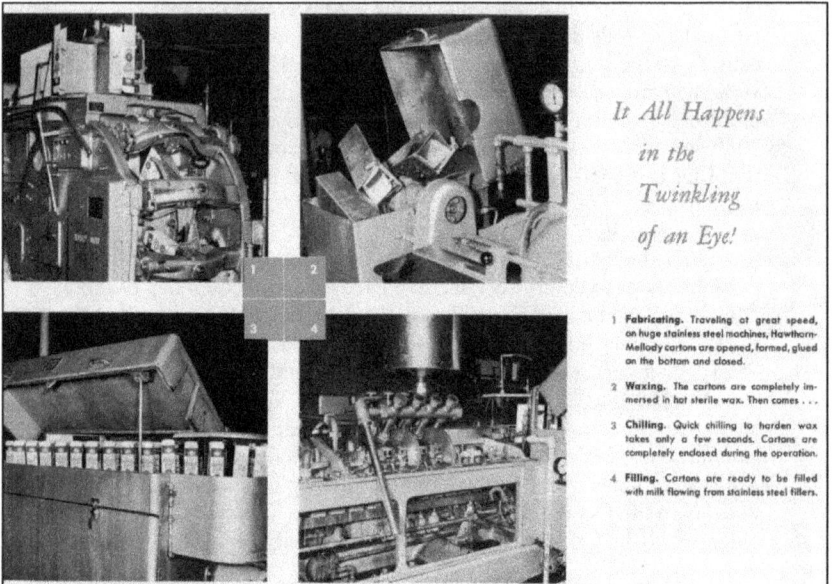

Figure 17. Postcard from the Hawthorn Melody Dairy on Chicago Ave. (Courtesy of J. Byrne from the Cuneo Museum).

Figure 18. Industrial alley between Chicago Avenue and Rice St. (Photo by Mark Bouman).

In terms of size and diversity the larger industrial zone of the neighborhood was located along the Belt Line from Chicago Ave. north to North Ave. There were actually two corridors of factories, one west of the tracks and the other east of the tracks (Figure 19). The west corridor is not considered part of the immediate neighborhood, but mention of some of the larger complexes is warranted.   In the vicinity of Iowa and Kilpatrick was a plant that produced the food flavor enhancer Accent. Just west of the Belt Line at 4647 W. Augusta Blvd. was the plastic sheeting manufacturer Warp's Plastic (This plant originated in 1924). The Leaf Candy Co., makers of Rainblo gumballs, jellied spearmint leaves, Whoppers malted milk balls, and other popular confections, occupied a square-block multi-story building at the southeast corner of Cicero Avenue and Division Street. On occasion the neighborhood was treated to sweet emanations from the plants exhaust stacks. Directly across the street from Leaf was the large complex of railroad switch and heavy equipment (e.g., graders and loaders) maker Pettibone Mulliken.

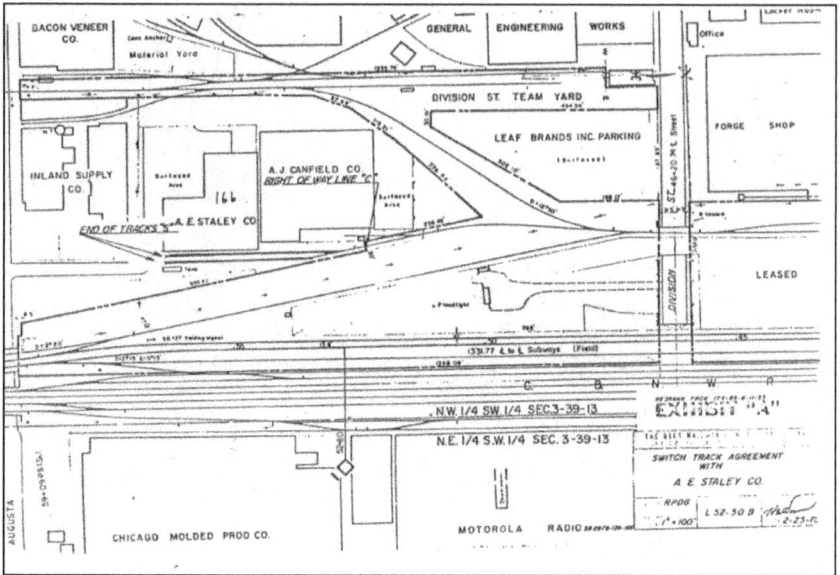

Figure 19. Copy of Belt Railway Switch Track Agreement Map. Note locations of Chicago Molded Products and Leaf Candy parking lot. (Courtesy R. Gelder, The Belt Railway Company of Chicago).

Industries east of the Belt Railway were in the neighborhood as defined in this study. No attempt is made here to catalog each and every plant as several closed down in the study period and other companies moved in. Rather, a sampling is provided to illustrate the diversified nature of this zone.

The 4400 block of West Rice St. (Figure 20) had several small industries like Paragon Spring Co. on the south side of the street. The north side of block was largely residential. This type of land use pattern was common at the time in many parts of Chicago. The Bowman Dairy Co. which delivered milk and other products right to your door as late as 1965 had a distributor at 4349 W. Iowa St.

Motorola (which began as the Galvin Manufacturing Corporation) had been located in a seven-story building on Harrison St. just a few blocks west of the Loop. In 1937 the company built a modern factory

32

and offices at 4545 W. Augusta Blvd. (Figures 21 & 22). The company chose the site particularly because it was in a largely residential area that could supply labor (Bruegmann, 1993). The original blue and white terra cotta building had 85,000 square feet of space. Within a decade or so, the plant had expanded to almost 500,000 square feet through the purchase and/or lease of nearby facilities. Through the 1960s, a large part of the business was in the manufacture of radios, televisions, and various mobile communications devices. Motorola radio equipment was used by the National Aeronautics and Space Administration (NASA).

Figure 20. Industries on the 4400 block of Rice Street. (Photo by Mark Bouman).

Across the street from Motorola was Chicago Molded Products. There were a number of industries located along Kolmar and Kilbourn Avenues from Augusta north to Haddon Ave. A few examples are Black Swan and Gottlieb. The Black Swan Manufacturing Co. at 4540 W. Thomas St. dates back to 1928 when chemical salesman Harry Lichten started The Industrial Paint and Varnish Co. By the 1960s, Black Swan was concentrating most of its manufacture in the area of plumbing materials such as putties, caulks, and wax gaskets. Gottlieb, a manufacturer of arcade games such as pinball machines and electromechanical bowling tables, had a large one-story plant on Haddon and Kostner.

The west side of Kostner Avenue from Division to North Avenue was lined with several sizeable industrial plants. Rembrandt Lamp Manufacturing was located at 4500 W. Division. About one-half block north at 1238 N. Kostner was the Universal Form Clamp factory.

Figure 21. Front entrance of Galvin Manufacturing Corporation (Motorola) headquarters and manufacturing facility, 4545 West Augusta Blvd., Chicago, circa 1940 (© Motorola, Inc., Heritage Services and Archives. Reproduced with permission).

Figure 22. Parking lot behind Motorola (Photo courtesy of P. Lucnik)

Stewart-Warner, maker of tachometers and other automotive instrumentation, had a satellite plant at 1300. Pyle National, manufacturer of railway signals, was located at 1334. Zenith Radio had a large plant on Kostner at Hirsch.

Helene Curtis Industries, maker of shampoos and related products had a large plant on North Avenue and Kostner (Figure 23). Nearly 1000 people worked at the facility. In October 1963 there was an explosion at the plant that killed one person and injured almost 200 employees.

Smaller concentrations of manufacturers, both big and small, could be found scattered throughout the neighborhood. Land-use along Grand Avenue was a mixture of commercial and industrial activities. Examples of industries dispersed along this thoroughfare were Abcotype Stamp Manufacturers at 4101 W. Grand, Apex Wire at 4158, Owen Welding at 4301, and Action Diamond Tool at 4545.

Figure 23. Helene Curtis plant on North Avenue and Kostner (Courtesy of Stephen M. Scalzo Collection).

One large industry was the Dudek & Bock Spring Manufacturing Co. located on Grand Avenue near Keystone (Figure 24). The company was founded by Joseph Dudek and Stanley Bock in 1946 in a small storefront on Damen Avenue. Within a few years they outgrew that location and purchased a building on Fulton Street, but that one also quickly proved inadequate. In 1954, Dudek and Bock moved to the new plant on Grand Avenue and through the years expanded that facility to 100,000 square feet. The plant employed 300 during the 1960s. Some of their customers were Kelsey Hayes, General Electric and several General Motors Divisions. With their business growing, the company relocated in 1970 to an even larger facility at 5100 W. Roosevelt Road.

Figure 24. Dudek & Bock Spring Mfg. Co. on Grand Avenue. (Courtesy Stephen M. Scalzo Collection).

There were several industries found on the largely commercial Division Street. There were two large industrial laundries, Rainbow at 4307 and Supreme at 4224 W. Division Street. The air around these plants always seemed to be warm and a hint of a freshly-starched linen smell lingered on the sidewalk (Source: oral histories). Both operations also had commercial shops serving the general public. A little further east at 4118 W. Division the aroma of lumber and wood shavings wafted out from the Supreme Casket Shell Company. Two other small plants on the street were Machinery Designing Co. at 4344 and Star Steel and Wire at 4425.

With all the industrial activity in and about the neighborhood, it is not surprising that several trucking and cartage companies had facilities in the area. One of the larger of these was Grane Trucking Co. at 4459 W. Division St. Grane served the Midwestern United States as a regional common and contract carrier. By 1970, the company had outgrown the

Division St. terminal and moved to a 14-acre site at 1001 South Laramie Avenue.

Figure 25. Grane Transportation trailer. (Photo courtesy of Brian Kuchay).

The neighborhood was in Chicago's "Outer Zone" of manufacturing as described by Reinemann (1960). This zone extends from Western Avenue to the western city limits. Reinemann found that, despite the overall suburbanization trend from 1941-1950, the Outer Zone had a net gain of 88 plants during the period suggesting that the area was still attractive for industry. As the 1960s progressed the neighborhood's industrial base was quite stable even though a few plants, most notably Salerno Bakery, did relocate to the suburbs. In the 1970s several more plants left the neighborhood. Some like Motorola went to the suburbs, but others like Dudek and Bock moved to larger facilities in other parts of the Outer Belt. This exodus was in part balanced by new companies coming into the neighborhood. For example, Playskool, a manufacturer of children's toys, moved into the Motorola complex and employed over 1,000 people. Playskool remained at that location until the mid-1980s when its parent company Hasbro Toys closed the plant.

Figure 26. In 2009, some of the factory buildings along N. Kostner Ave. await new owners. (Photo by Mark Bouman).

CHAPTER 6:

COMMERCIAL ACTIVITIES

A wide array of goods and services were conveniently available in and near the neighborhood. There were a number of little grocery, candy, and sundries stores scattered throughout the area on both the commercial and residential streets. People did not have to travel very far for everyday consumer staples. For more specialized goods and services, however, the shopper would have to go to the area's main commercial streets.

The locations, sizes, and number of establishments in the neighborhood can be analyzed with an adaptation of central place theory. Central place theory was proposed by the economic geographer Walter Christaller in 1933 in an attempt to explain the size, function, and spacing of cities as central places that provided goods and services to the surrounding population. Christaller characterized goods and services as being low-order or high-order. Lower-order goods are items such as food and common household products that need to be purchased frequently and are generally of nominal cost. Higher-order goods are things like automobiles, furniture, and appliances that are purchased rather infrequently. The threshold or population needed to make a particular type of establishment prosperous, is quite small for lower-order items like groceries and daily newspapers and is high for big-ticket items such as refrigerators.

By applying an adaptation of the theory to Chicago and the neighborhood of this study, the top of the central place hierarchy would be the Loop. In the 1960s the downtown was still the city's primate shopping district anchored by a number of multi-storied flagship department stores like Marshall Field, Sears Roebuck, Carson-Pirie-Scott, Wiebolt's, Goldblatt's, and Montgomery Ward. The Loop was, and still is, home to numerous specialty stores purveying a wide range of consumer and shopping goods. In addition, the Loop was the financial and personal services center for the city. It was a first-order central place and its catchment area was the entire metropolitan region. People from the neighborhood would on occasion, when necessary or as a diversion, patronize Loop establishments, but most lower-order and some higher-order goods and services could be obtained locally.

The next level of the central place hierarchy would be occupied by the major commercial districts of the neighborhoods. Just about every Chicago neighborhood in the 1960s had a thriving commercial district situated at a busy intersection. For the West Side neighborhood in this study, that intersection was that of North Avenue and Pulaski Road (Figures 27, 28, & 29). The intensity of commercial activity was greatest at the intersection where Pioneer Bank (in 2009 Banco Popular), Walgreen's, F.W. Woolworth, and Andes Candies occupied the corner lots. Nearby along North Avenue was an assortment of vendors such as Morrie Mages sporting goods/Community Discount Store, the Crawford Department Store, Ferndell's Restaurant, Izen Shoes, a DeMars restaurant, Ursin Shoes, Blumer's Bakery, Jim's Hobby Shop, Vollendorf's Fish and Delicatessen, Baskind Radio and Jewelry, Fannie May Candies, and several men's and women's clothiers . On Pulaski behind the bank was Andersen's record shop (where customers could listen to the records before making their purchase decision), and behind the Walgreen's was a Dell Farm Supermarket. A block west of Pulaski at North and Keystone was Wishnick's Prescription Center with physician and dentist offices in the back. Several large furniture stores such as Kral's, Ben Mozinski's and Peterson's, as well the catalog house First Distributors which sold jewelry, watches, radios, and small appliances were located in the vicinity of 4200 W. The Moeller-Halleman Funeral Home was at 4138 W. North Avenue. Further west at 4250 was the Lion's Hotel which also had banquet and meeting room facilities. The district also had several recreational venues such as the Pioneer Bowl, Tiffin Theater, Lion's Bowling Lanes, and Regina nightclub (Figure 30).

A number of attorneys, accountants, physicians, and dentists had offices located on the second and third floors of the commercial buildings. A branch of the Chicago Public Library was located on Pulaski across the alley from the Andes/Ferndell's building (In the late 1960s the library relocated to a storefront in the 4000 block of W. North Avenue. The neighborhood U.S. Post Office was located on the southwest corner of North and Harding Ave.

The Norford Hotel (Figure 31) at 1508 N. Pulaski Road opened in the 1920s. Hotels like the Norford and Windsor (Chicago Ave. at Cicero) were a common feature in just about every Chicago neighborhood's major shopping district. From its opening until the mid-1960s, the Norford was utilized by businessmen traveling to the neighborhood and on occasion by out-of-town relatives visiting family in the area. The hotel had a small ballroom and banquet facility on its lower level where wedding receptions, business meetings, and other affairs were held. By the late 1960s the clientele was changing as the regional importance of the commercial district was waning. Also by that time, travelling businessmen were more apt to seek

Figure 27. Northwest corner of Pulaski Road and North Avenue in 1967. The Pioneer Bank building is on the corner and the record shop is seen on the far right. (Photo courtesy of Stephen M. Scalzo collection).

Figure 28 . North side of 3900 block of West North Avenue in 1967. (Photo courtesy of Stephen M. Scalzo collection).

Figure 29. Andes Candies Store # 8 on North and Pulaski. (Photo courtesy of Kathy Maass of Tootsie Roll Industries).

Figure 30. Regina Inn on North Avenue in 1967. On the far right is First Distributors. (Photo courtesy of Stephen M. Scalzo collection).

lodgings in the Loop or near O'Hare airport. As of January 2009, the Norford still stands and today serves as an S.R.O. (Single Resident Occupance) residential hotel serving lower-income people.

Figure 31. The Norford Hotel at 1508 N. Pulaski (Courtesy Gordon McAlpin).

One can also include in the North/Pulaski district, the businesses located in the vicinity of Grand Avenue and Pulaski. Grand Avenue is a diagonal street that originates near the downtown and continues out into the near suburbs.

Jimmy's Red Hots (Figure 32) has been a fixture on the northwest corner of Grand and Pulaski since 1954. This little hot dog stand has provided commuters and neighborhood residents alike with simple fare like Chicago-style Vienna Beef ® hot dogs (No ketchup!), hand-cut French fries, and little bunches of steamed Supreme ® tamales all at a very reasonable cost (29 cents for a hot dog and fries in 1960). Even today, some former neighborhood residents will make an occasional pilgrimage to Jimmy's.

Figure 32. Pulaski and Grand. Jimmy's Red Hots is on the left. Behind the hot dog stand is a CTA electrical substation providing power for the trolley buses. (Steve Zabel photo, courtesy of Joe Testagrose Collection).

Across from Jimmy's was a new car dealership, Motor King Rambler. The location of this enterprise is interesting because it was slightly off the beaten path. About one mile east on Grand Avenue was a concentration of new car dealerships—Jim Moran Ford, Mr. Norm's Grand-Spaulding Dodge (Figure 33), Grand-Central Chrysler Plymouth, and Foreman Cadillac. New car dealerships often concentrate in space in order to take advantage of agglomeration economies (cost savings from clustering). Motor King Rambler was a small dealership selling an independent rather than a "Big 3" model and may have needed lower overhead so it used a lower cost location, but still one that had a good deal of exposure. Both Grand Ave. and Pulaski were major CTA bus routes and the location was just a block and half south of the North/Pulaski shopping district. Around 1970, Motor King switched to the Lincoln/Mercury brand and by the end of that decade closed its doors. In fact, the aforementioned agglomeration of dealerships near Grand and Homan were all gone by that time, as the customer base was shifting to the suburbs.

Figure 33. Mr. Norm's Grand Spaulding Dodge circa 1968. (T. Dzik collection).

Also in the vicinity of Grand and Pulaski were a number of other small businesses such as taverns and restaurants. A modest used car lot was located across from Motor King and a muffler and brake shop was located in the 3900 block of W. Grand Avenue.

Jewel Food Stores (Figure 34) opened a new supermarket on the north side of Grand Ave. near Karlov around 1962. This was the largest supermarket in the neighborhood as its complex occupied a full city block with an ample parking lot. The arrival of this large store negatively impacted some of the small independent "corner" grocery stores on the neighborhood's residential streets because Jewel possessed great advantages in variety and price. A few little stores closed within a year or two of the new Jewel.

The North/Pulaski community district's size and make-up could rival that of any American small-town (e.g., 50,000 population) Central Business District of the period. Yet, no national or regional department store was represented in the North/Pulaski concentration. The closest such store would have been the Goldblatt's department store on Madison and Pulaski in a larger neighborhood commercial district over a mile away from the neighborhood. Residents would on occasion venture southward to Madison

Figure 34. Jewel-Osco Supermarket on Grand Avenue and Karlov (Photo adapted from Stephen M. Scalzo collection).

Street to take advantage of that area's somewhat larger array of goods, but these visits became less frequent as the West Garfield Park community's African-American population increased.

The commercial strips along Division Street and along Pulaski Road from Division south to Chicago Avenue can be thought of as the third level of the central place hierarchy. The variety of goods and services along these stretches was more modest than that found in the second level. With a few exceptions such as the Kolssak Funeral Home (Figure 35) and Cesar's Italian Restaurant (the neighborhood's fanciest dining), most businesses were dispensing lower-order goods and services. There were several groceries and delicatessens such as Joe's Quality Meats, Leo's Bakery and

Delicatessen,and Austermuehle's Certified. An interesting sideline of A-Affliliated Liquors at 4211 W. Division was a small phonograph record section stocking current Top 40 45 RPMs and Easy Listening LPs by artists such as Jerry Vale and Perry Como. Figure 36 illustrates the location of commercial activities along Division Street. Unlike the dense concentration of establishments in the North/Pulaski area, commercial ventures along Division Street were largely interspersed among residential and industrial land uses.

The Pulaski Road commercial strip south of Grand Avenue was also occupied primarily by stores dispensing lower-order goods, but there were also a few specialty shops. From Kamerling Avenue southward to Division Street some noteworthy establishments were Steve's Pizzeria, AAA Board Up, Marie's Beauty Shop, Crystal Bakery, York Urban Service Station, Addante Florist, and Patrician Plastics. From Division down to Chicago Avenue, some significant businesses were Livia's Pizzeria, Landsman Pharmacy, Standard Lumber, Tennenbaum Hardware, Boulevard Bakery, Tony's Boulevard Tavern, Marshall's Phillips 66, Carl Stockholm Cleaners, Louie's Cities Service gas station, Joe Cannata's Meat Market, and Jim and Al's Pizzeria & Lounge. Just as on Division Street, these commercial activities were interspersed among residential and light industrial land-uses.

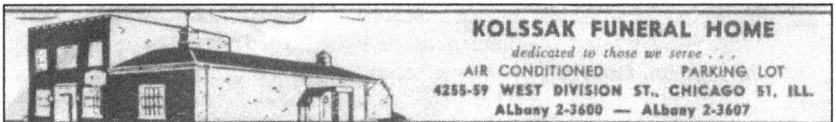

KOLSSAK FUNERAL HOME
dedicated to those we serve . . .
AIR CONDITIONED   PARKING LOT
4255-59 WEST DIVISION ST., CHICAGO 51, ILL.
ALbany 2-3600 — ALbany 2-3607

Figure 35. Advertisement for Kolssak Funeral Home from the St. Francis of Assisi Church bulletin (Courtesy of P. Lucnik).

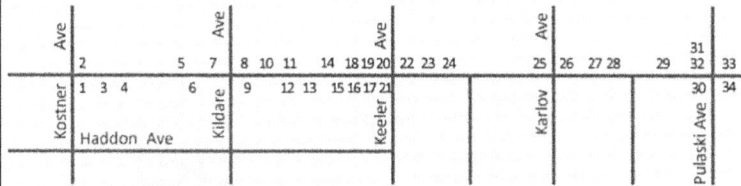

Commercial Establishments Along Division Street Circa 1965

1	J. Zydiak, MD
2	Division-Kostner Standard Oil Gas Station
3	Division-Kostner Currency Exchange
4	Baker's Lounge
5	Joe's Cleaners & Alterations
6	Rainbow Laundry
7	Stoltman Pharmacy
	C.R. Choulnard, MD
8	Tom's Pizza Palace
9	Kolssak Funeral Home
10	Woodway Laundry
11	Joe's Quality Food Market
12	Bureau of Surveys
13	Val Poretta & Torti Cement Contractors
14	Supreme Laundry and Dry Cleaners
15	Club Whirlabout Tavern
16	Adam's Hardware
17	A-Afilliated Liquors
18	Phil's Barber Shop
19	Debra-Lynn Shop
20	Kildare Florist
21	Sam Caccavale Sundries & Confectionery
22	Division-Keeler Certified Grocery
23	Leo's Bakery & Delicatessen
24	Reich Paint Co.
25	Fran's Delicatessen
26	Austermuehle Certified Grocery
27	Plaza Beauty Shop
28	Prudential Insurance Co.
29	May and Speh Tabulating
30	Cesar's Italian Restaurant & Lounge
31	Addante Florist
32	Patrician Plastics
	L.J. Schwartz, DDS
	M.I. Schwartz, DDS
33	Division-Pulaski Standard Oil Gas Station
34	Harold's Snack Shop

Figure 36. Commercial establishments along Division St. (Cartography by Karla Sanders).

The fourth level of the neighborhood's central place hierarchy would be clusters of 3 or 4 commercial establishments in close proximity to one another on an otherwise residential street. There were two such central places in the neighborhood. One was at the intersection of Cortez and Kildare where Walter Bryk's Grocery and Meats, Rogala's Candy and Sundries, the K.C. Tap tavern, and Ripka's Shoe Repair (Figure 37) formed a tiny commercial district. Another small cluster was along Thomas St. just east of Kostner Avenue where the Harmony Hall and Tavern, Walter Cygan's Candy Store, Majer Greenhouse and Florist, and the Little Lady Grocery were located.

Figure 37. Interior of Ripka's Shoe Repair (Photo courtesy of Joe Ripka).

The fifth tier of the hierarchy would be the stand-alone shops which could be found on most of the neighborhood's residential streets. Almost all of these were little grocery stores (such as Peterka's at 4258 W. Iowa, Ben Rusin's Walton St. Foods at 4405 W. Walton, and Olga Michalec's Delicatessen at 1400 N. Kildare) or taverns (such as Alice's Firefly at 4258 W. Thomas and Albina Panik's at 4349 W. Iowa). There were a few exceptions. Paragon Cleaners was at 4257 W. Augusta Blvd. Stella's Dry

Goods (Figures 38 & 39) which mainly sold women's and children's clothing and accessories (as well as Communion dresses and suits) occupied a corner storefront at 4300 W. Haddon in 1962. Like a few other neighborhood businesses, Stella's accepted payment of telephone, electric, and natural gas bills as a convenient service to their neighborhood customers. Another notable stand-alone business was the Plichta Funeral

Figure 38. Advertisement for Stella's Dry Goods from St. Francis of Assisi Church bulletin (Courtesy of P. Lucnik).

Figure 39. Storefront at 4300 W. Haddon in 2006 (T. Dzik Collection).

Home at 4348 W. Walton St. (Figure 40). This mortuary that opened in 1949 was strategically located just a few hundred feet from St. Francis of Assisi Church and about a block away from Sts. Cyril and Methodius Church.

Figure 40. Plichta Funeral Home in 1963. (Photo courtesy of Sharon Quigley).

At the beginning of the decade there were 21 small grocery stores in the neighborhood. By that time, they were largely a throwback to earlier days when many people did not have refrigerators and needed to purchase small amounts of perishable food product almost daily. As the 1960s progressed, nine of these little groceries had exited the business. The arrival of large chain supermarkets and the increasing mobility of the population were the prime factors in the demise of these mom-and-pop enterprises. They were going the way of the milkman. Bowman Dairy Co. from River Forest, Illinois had a distributor at 4349 W. Iowa. Early morning home milk delivery in the neighborhood lasted until the late 1960s.

It is interesting to note that there were no business establishments of any type located on Kedvale, Karlov, and Keystone Avenues north of Augusta and south of Division. This was the area of the Pillars of Kedvale and the absence of shops may be related to the original plan that this area was to be an exclusive gated residential community.

Some residents of the neighborhood also utilized the commercial district on Chicago Avenue just east of Pulaski Road. The district was outside of the neighborhood as delineated in this study, but it was especially important to local Italian-Americans as a number of ethnic specialty shops were located there. There were also a few retail and entertainment establishments such as the Alamo Theater that were frequented by residents of all backgrounds.

Figure 41. Some of the neighborhood storefronts like this one at Hirsch and Karlov still function in 2009 in the same way that they did in the 1960s. (Photo by Mark Bouman).

CHAPTER 7:

CHURCHES

The churches of the neighborhood were perhaps the most integral parts of the community. Not only did they serve the religious needs of the populace, they also provided options for socialization and education. The majority of the neighborhood's populace was Catholic which is understandable given the area's ethnic composition and the two Catholic parishes were large. There were only two Protestant churches in the neighborhood. The locations of the churches are shown in Figure 42.

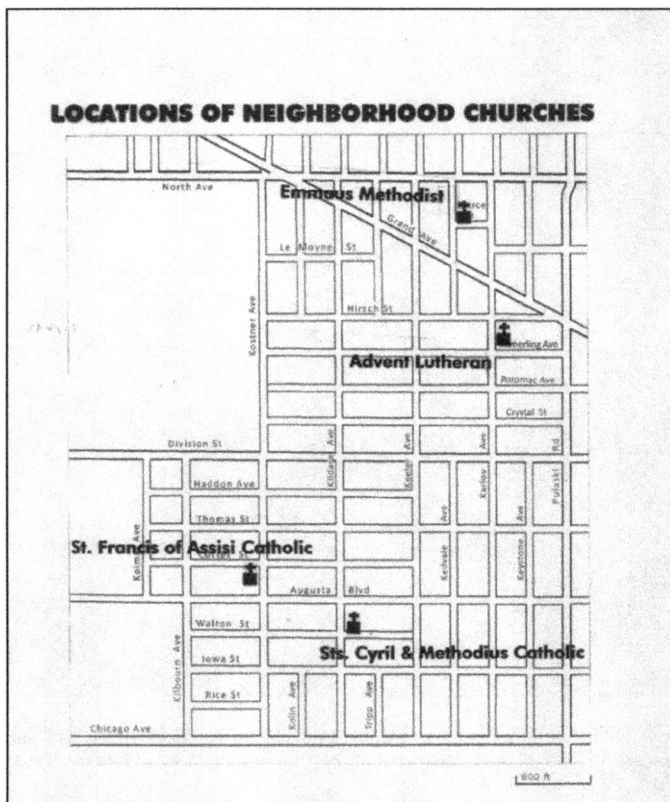

Figure 42. Locations of the neighborhood's four churches. (Cartography by Karla Sanders and Tony Dzik).

St. Francis of Assisi Roman Catholic

The largest parish in the neighborhood was the St. Francis of Assisi parish. This Roman Catholic church was, and as of 2009, still is located at the intersection of Kostner Ave. and Augusta Blvd. The parish was founded in 1909 to serve the needs of about 160 Polish and Slovakian families that were living in the neighborhood. In the United States, the Catholic dioceses permitted immigrant groups to develop their own exclusive parishes (Bigott, 2001). The original church building (Figures 43 & 44) located at 4422 W. Walton St. was dedicated July 10, 1910. In 1912 an elementary school was established. Up until the early 1950s, instruction was in English and Polish. By 1925, the school's enrollment topped 400. The original church building was a multi-purpose facility with the worship space on the main level, classrooms on the second level, and a parish hall in the basement. In 1956 a new rectory (Figure 45) was constructed at 932 N. Kostner. The architecture was reflective of the Frank Lloyd Wright school of design.

Figure 43. Original St. Francis of Assisi Church on W. Walton St. (Photo courtesy of Michael Goc).

Figure 44. Interior of the original church, circa 1956 (Photo courtesy of P. Lucnik).

Figure 45. St. Francis of Assisi Rectory (Photo courtesy of P. Lucnik).

By the mid-1950s it had become apparent that the old church building had become inadequate for the burgeoning parish and a fund-raising campaign commenced with the goal of a modern edifice. The new church (Figure 46) at the corner of Kostner Ave. and Augusta Blvd. was dedicated in April 1959. At that time the parish rolls listed approximately 800 families, a number that would hold steady through the 1960s. With a new church in service, the old church building was remodeled, expanding classroom and meeting space.

Figure 46. New St. Francis of Assisi Church (Photo courtesy of Michael Goc).

Figure 47. St. Francis schoolchildren on the way to church in the 1960s (Courtesy of P. Lucnik)

Throughout the 1960s St. Francis had five priests in residence. The sanctuary was a busy place. Six Masses were said each Sunday and two of them, the 7 A.M. and 10 A.M., were in the Polish language. On most weekdays there were four Masses offered. In addition to the Masses, a number of special services were frequently held. Stations of the Cross, Exposition of the Blessed Sacrament, Litanies, and other liturgies were held on Sunday afternoons and on weekday evenings. The parish hall also was humming throughout the decade. School plays, Holy Communion breakfasts, various bazaars and bingos, and Saturday movie showings for the parish's children were just a few of the diversions presented there.

The parish school closed in 1988. As of 2009, St. Francis of Assisi church still operates serving a small community of Hispanic-American and African-American Catholics in the neighborhood.

Sts. Cyril and Methodius Roman Catholic

Located on Kildare near Walton St, just a block away from St. Francis, was the Sts. Cyril and Methodius Roman Catholic church. Named for the missionaries who brought Christianity to the Slavic peoples, this parish was organized in 1913 to meet the needs of the growing number of Slovaks on the West Side. Up to that time, the Slovak people of the neighborhood had been worshipping at the nearby Polish church. Ground was broken for the church in July 1915. Like St. Francis, the Slovak church was a multi-purpose building having worship space on the main level and a grammar school on the upper floor.

The parish in the mid-1960s was served by two resident priests and four Masses were said each Sunday. Worship was in English and Slovak. Special services such as Forty Hours Devotions and the Way of the Cross were also part of St. Cyril's religious life. The parish sponsored a number of organizations such as the Holy Name Society and the St. Elizabeth's Society that were involved in religious activities and parish fund-raising.

It is estimated that the parish served about 600-900 faithful during most of the 1960s. As the number of Slovaks in the area never approached those of the Poles, Sts. Cyril and Methodius parish membership was a little more ethnically diverse that that of St. Francis. St. Cyril's location may have played a part in this as there were more Irish- and Italian-American Catholics living at the eastern end of the neighborhood than in the immediate vicinity of St. Francis church. By the mid-1970s, only about one-half of the parish families were Slovak (Koenig, 1980).

By the end of the 1960s, parish membership was declining and the elementary school ceased to be in 1972. The church soldiered on until 1987 when the archdiocese of Chicago closed the parish.

Figure 48. Sts. Cyril and Methodius Roman Catholic Church (Photo courtesy of Sr. Theresa Lesnak).

Figure 49. Part of the St. Cyril and Methodius Elementary School graduating class of 1963 (Photo courtesy of Sharon Quigley).

Advent Lutheran

Advent English Lutheran Church (Figure 50) was at 1345 N. Karlov. The 2 ½ story church and parish-house building was erected in 1915. The parish was organized in 1912 to serve Lutheran Christians in the area. Many of the early congregants were of Norwegian descent. Their community had been slowly expanding westward from Humboldt Park. They were joined in worship by German-American Lutherans already living in the vicinity. Advent also served a small dispersed population of Swedes. The presence of Scandinavian ethnics in the area is evidenced by the local public elementary school which was named for the noted Swedish physicist Alfred Nobel. Advent was not only a religious center, but also hosted community functions such as Boy Scout troop meetings. Typical of churches in areas with changing demographics, the church has gone through several reincarnations since a 1973 merger with Hope Epiphany Lutheran. In 2009, building houses the Mission of Christ Church.

Emmaus United Methodist Church

Emmaus United Methodist Church (Figure 51) was located on the corner of Pierce and Kedvale. Its congregation was composed mainly of persons of Anglo-Irish, Swedish, and German descent. As the demographics of the neighborhood shifted in the 1980s, the church became the Creciendo al Ritmo del Pueblo United Methodist Church. That Spanish-speaking congregation outgrew the church building and moved to larger facilities in the Hermosa Community Area. The church and parsonage in 2009 are owned by the United Methodist Chicago Home Missionary and Church Extension Society.

Figure 50. Advent English Lutheran Church at 1345 N. Karlov (Photo courtesy of Joel Thoreson, Evangelical Lutheran Church in America Archive).

Figure 51. Former Emmaus Methodist Church Building (T. Dzik Collection).

Neighboring Churches

Mention must be made of two Roman Catholic churches located just outside of the neighborhood as defined in this monograph. St. Philomena Church at Kedvale and Cortland was originally founded to serve German Catholic families in the Hermosa Community Area and in the 1960s, some neighborhood residents, particularly those living close to North Avenue, were parishioners. Our Lady of the Angels Church at 3800 W. Iowa was started in 1894 to serve Irish Catholics living west of Humboldt Park. By the mid-1950s, Italian-Americans made-up about 40-50% of its congregation. In 2009, the church is home to a Baptist congregation. More details about OLA can be found in Chapter 9.

Figure 52. Bells of St. Francis of Assisi Church in 2009. (Photo by Mark Bouman).

CHAPTER 8:

RECREATION AND SOCIALIZATION

For many residents of the neighborhood the Catholic churches were major foci for fun and social interaction. This was common in most northern cities and was part of what McGreevy (1996) described as "a specifically Catholic style of merging neighborhood and religious organized life." Organizations such as the St. Ann's Club, Knights of Cyrillian Guild, Holy Name Society, Rosary Sodality, and other church groups, in addition to their religious activities, held assorted amusements like bazaars, ham raffles, dances, and bingo. For a few years, St. Francis of Assisi parish annually held a week-long full-blown carnival complete with rides, games, and polka bands. These affairs were well-attended by parishioners and non-parishioners, young and old alike.

The 31st Ward Polish-American Citizens Club (a misnomer as the membership also included Slovaks, Italians, and others) was a political and social organization that occasionally sponsored polka dances, picnics, and other diversions. Many of their affairs were held at Harmony Hall located on the corner of Kostner Ave. and Thomas St. Harmony Hall was a multi-purpose facility that hosted wedding receptions, funeral dinners, union meetings, polka parties, and, twice a year served as a polling place. With regard to polka music, many well-known Chicago area bands like the Ampol Aires and the Harmony Kings played at the hall.

A number of younger men in the neighborhood were members of a social club called the Windsors (name taken from the Windsor Hotel that was located just a few blocks from the area at Cicero and Chicago Avenues). The Windsors fielded an amateur team that played 16-inch softball, a game that is essentially unique to Chicago. The game which became popular in the 1920s was well-suited for Chicago's small neighborhood parks and cinder-covered school playgrounds as the batted ball didn't travel very far even with a mighty swat. Equipment requirements are modest—a ball and a bat (no fielder mitts needed)—and that made the game accessible to people of all economic backgrounds and age groups. The Windsors also had a youth basketball program. Many of the neighborhood taverns sponsored local softball teams that played at local Augusta Park and at Lafollette Park in the neighboring Austin community area.

No less than 22 taverns existed in the neighborhood's 40 square-block territory (Figure 53). While some residents may have frequented more than one establishment with regularity, most folks had a special place. Some of the taverns were patronized by people who lived in the immediate vicinity of the place while others had larger catchment areas. The clientele also varied somewhat. For example, the KC Trap's regular customers tended to be of Slovak descent and many of them were in the 20s and 30s. The Alibi Inn on North Avenue near Keeler served as a gathering place for folks transplanted from rural southern Illinois and Appalachia. The patrons of Ed's Tavern across from St. Francis church tended to be of Polish descent. On occasion Chicago Blackhawks professional hockey players would stop by Ed's. For a few years, a bungalow behind Ed's was rented seasonally by Blackhawks winger Ken Wharram and Chicago Cubs baseballer Earl Averill (Figures 54 & 55). On occasion, Wharram and other Blackhawks would go to Augusta Park to informally conduct skating and hockey lessons for neighborhood kids. Taverns like Noga's on Thomas near Kilbourn and the Crystal Tap (Figure 56) on Kostner and Crystal were neighborhood saloons, but because of their proximity to the neighborhood industries they also served lunches for the workers.

The local movie palace was the Tiffin Theater at 4051 W. North Ave. (Figure 57) Designed by the architectural firm Meyer Fridstein & Co, it opened in 1922. At night on North Ave, the warm inviting lights of the theater's marquee were visible from several blocks away. Even in the 1960s the interior was still grand—plushy red velvety seats and golden filigree on the walls. The Tiffin presented double features. Second-run Elvis Presley, Disney, and werewolf films were common fare, but on occasion there would be first-run movies like "The Blue Max" (1966 film starring George Peppard and Ursula Andress). Like most theaters of that era, the Tiffin had a large stage and in 1965 the British rock-and-roll band The Dave Clark Five made a personal appearance promoting their movie "Having a Wild Weekend". The Tiffin continued operating until the mid-1980s. In its last days it was featuring Spanish-language films as a service to the area's new demographics. By then the building was showing its age and it was demolished in the 1990s.

Figure 53. Locations of Neighborhood Taverns (Cartography by Karla Sanders and Tony Dzik).

Figure 54. Ken Wharram Topps' Hockey Card and Earl Averill's Topps' Baseball Card. Wharram and Averill lived seasonally in a rented bungalow behind Ed's Tavern. (T. Dzik collection).

Figure 55. Bungalow behind the former Ed's Tavern on N. Kostner Ave. that was rented seasonally by Chicago Cubs and Blackhawks players. (Photo by Mark Bouman).

Figure 56. The now-shuttered Crystal Tap at the corner of Crystal and Kostner (Photo by Mark Bouman).

Figure 57. View east on North Avenue in the late 1950s. The Tiffin Theater is on the far left. (Photo Courtesy of Jerry Kasper).

Another popular diversion was bowling. There were three bowling alley establishments on the neighborhood's periphery. All had special promotions. For example, the Pioneer Bowl (Figure 58) on Pulaski near North Ave. had a "red pin" deal. If the #1 pin was red and a strike was rolled, the bowler was awarded a free game. The Pioneer also had a billiards room. The Lions Bowl was located on North Ave. near Keeler. This bowling alley was part of a larger complex that also had meeting rooms and banquet facilities. People at the south end of the neighborhood might frequent G & L Bowling and Liquors on the southeast corner of Chicago Avenue and Pulaski Road.

Figure 58. Pioneer Bowl on Pulaski near North Ave. (Courtesy of Gordon McAlpin)

Young people and children could often be found at one of the neighborhood's three playgrounds. Augusta Park on Augusta Blvd and Kilbourn was a small city park/playground that opened in 1932. An ample concrete sandbox, several sets of swings, and a slide were attractive to the area's youngsters. A baseball diamond with backstop saw heavy use during the warm seasons. In mid-winter Park District employees would flood the diamond and an ice skating rink would develop in the subfreezing Chicago temperatures. Although the Park District forbade hockey on the playground rinks, impromptu games would materialize at off-peak hours, and sometimes even after-hours. The Augusta Park field house was the site and many formal and informal ping pong (table tennis) matches.

Figure 59. Family time in Augusta Park circa 1963 (Photo courtesy of G. Lopatka)

Another playground and baseball diamond was located behind Orr School in the 4200 block of W. Cortez. It had a good complement of swings, parallel bars, monkey bars, and sandboxes. Like at Augusta Park, the ball field became a skating rink in late January. The field house at Orr was larger than the one at Augusta and would host Halloween parties and hot dog roasts for the neighborhood children. Sadly, the Orr playground and field house were demolished in the mid-1960s after plans were made to add-on several wings to the school building. Children residing north of Division St. would avail themselves of the facilities at Kedvale Park (Hirsch St. near Kedvale) which abutted Nobel School. This facility had playground equipment, basketball courts, a small field house, and a small playing field.

Although the neighborhood playgrounds had some small outdoor basketball courts and these saw some use, basketball was not nearly as popular as baseball and its variations.

There were some opportunities for musical and dance instruction in the area. One such establishment was the Harrison School of Dance on North Avenue and Kostner (Figure 60).

Figure 60. Activities circa 1963. Left is Harrison School of Dancing (Photo adapted from Stephen M. Scalzo Collection); Right is a neighborhood slugger (Courtesy of P. Lucnik).

Neighborhood children of earlier times may have occasionally visited the somewhat distant Garfield and Humboldt Parks. By the 1960s, however, most neighborhood parents would have strongly discouraged a visit. The Garfield Park area was experiencing a dramatic racial change and Humboldt Park was beginning to be perceived as being unsafe because of ethnic strife. Nonetheless, a handful of neighborhood kids in the 1960s had their first fishing experience at the Humboldt Park "lagoon"

Outside of a few programs run at the playgrounds, there were not many opportunities for organized play in the area. This lack of supervised play, however, did not deter children from having fun and it did not incline most to mischievous behavior.

71

A popular pastime for boys (and some girls) was the game of "Fast Pitching". All one needed for this two or four kid game was a baseball bat, a small rubber ball purchased from Rogala's or Wally's candy store, and a wall facing lots of open space. A strike zone would be drawn on the wall with chalk (sometimes paint) and the pitcher and batter would commence. Popular sites for such games were on the grounds of Nobel and Orr Schools, and in the factory parking lots on Cortez west of Kilbourn.. Another simple ball game played with a dime or quarter rubber ball was "hit-em-out". This game could be played solo or in pairs and was usually played in the alley by bouncing the ball against a garage wall and fielding it. In the autumn, impromptu games of street touch football might develop on a side street. Such games were generally of short duration, abruptly being disbanded when an adult would yell "Don cha kids got a playground? You wanna bust a car window or sumthin'!" Scavenging the neighborhood's alleys for returnable soda bottles and other treasures was an occasional diversion for some youngsters. Bringing the bottles to one of the little grocery or candy stores to get the 2 cent deposit sometimes was a challenge as the shopkeeper might carefully examine the bottle and declare that you didn't buy the soda from him. He might then suggest that you take it elsewhere or place it somewhere "where the sun doesn't shine."

Up until about late 1962 (when city ordinances changed), the weekly appearance of the junkman with his horse and wagon would be announced with his cry "Rags a Line! Rags a Line!"(He was actually intoning "Rags and old iron!"). Children would run to their alley gate to lay their eyes on the horse who often sported a threadbare fedora or ragged straw bowler (with holes cut out to accommodate the beast's ears). For some of us urban urchins, the junkman's horse was a little bit of country come to town.

For some teenagers, hanging about the school grounds smoking cigarettes and talking dirty helped pass the time. Others formed garage bands that attempted to play the rock-and-roll hits of the era. On almost any Saturday afternoon in 1966 in almost any residential alley one would hear the jangle of inexpensive Teisco electric guitars and the strained strains of "Gloria" and "Hang on Sloopy" resonating from the inside of some garage.

Most people in the neighborhood did not have air conditioning, so on sultry summer nights many adults and children would try to catch a little breeze while sitting on their front porches and steps. Others took a stroll to the candy store for a cold soda or an ice cream. Others walked to the Whirlabout tavern to get a cold Blatz or Meister Brau and catch a few innings of the Sox on TV. On the way there'd be conversations with the step-sitters. In this manner, people got caught up on all the neighborhood news.

Gardening was a diversion for many homeowners who had an ample backyard. Pretty flower beds and rose bushes were part of many backyard landscapes, but a portion of many yards was devoted to the cultivation of vegetables and fruits. Many homeowners had grown up in the Great Depression and/or had come to America from rural areas of Poland or Italy and they possessed the traits of practicality and frugality. Little plots of tomato and pepper plants were common as were backyard apple trees, especially in the census tract south of Division Street where there were more single-family and 2-flat homes. With so many residents engaged in "urban" agriculture, it is no surprise that there was a full-service greenhouse business (Z. Majer Florist and Greenhouse) occupying about 5 city lots in the 4300 block of W. Thomas St.

CHAPTER 9:

MISCELLEANOUS EVENTS, PEOPLE AND PLACES

BLIZZARD OF 1967

The meteorologists had forecast a snowfall of about 4 inches, a trifling amount for a January day in Chicago. In the "city that works" it would be a mild inconvenience. The snow began falling around 5 A.M. on Thursday, January 26, 1967. The morning commute was a bit dicey, but manageable for most people. By the noon hour, the snow was coming down steadily and the accumulation was beginning to be cause for concern. Many schools and some businesses dismissed early. By 3 P.M., many streets approached impassability as the wind was causing drifting. On streets such as California Ave. and Pulaski Road, electric trolley buses were mired in drifts or had become detached from the overhead wires after skidding. The evening rush-hour was tortuous and normal 40- minute commutes were this evening taking four or five hours. Downtown hotels were booked solid with stranded out-of-towners and Loop office workers. The snow continued through the night and didn't stop until 10 A.M. Friday. Total accumulation was 23 inches.

The city was engulfed and practically immobilized. More than 20,000 automobiles and 500 CTA buses were abandoned on the city streets and expressways. Giant snowdrifts blocked side streets and major thoroughfares alike. The city had been knocked to the canvas. But Chicagoans are a resilient tribe and by Saturday the city was stirring. The els and subways were back in full operation and buses were operating on 2/3 of the CTA routes. People were digging out throughout the city. By Sunday, the expressways had been cleared and O'Hare airport had reopened. City snow removal crews and private contractors worked around the clock. Monday's commutes were slow even with the schools remaining closed. By Tuesday the city was approaching normalcy. To the distress of most residents, Wednesday saw an additional four inches of snowfall. The city was prepared and the main arterials were kept quite clear. On Monday, February 8, another 8 inches fell, but the impact was modest. In eleven days almost 37 inches of snow had been recorded—the most snow on the ground at any time in the existence of the Chicago Weather Bureau.

Many neighborhood residents had a difficult time making it home from work on the evening of January 26. For some, the journey home involved circuitous routes riding a bus for a few blocks until it became stuck, then trudging through the streets for a bit until a kind motorist gave them a ride for a mile or so, and then more walking. More than a few stopped once or twice at a tavern or restaurant on the way for a warming drink.

On Friday and throughout the weekend neighbors banded together to clear snow from the streets, alleys, and sidewalks. On some blocks it was a festive affair with neighborhood women dispensing hot coffee, cocoa, and stronger beverages to shovelers while children sledded and constructed snow forts. Teenagers made a good deal of money digging out cars and clearing porches and walkways.

Many of the little groceries and candy stores in the neighborhood stayed open during the time of the city's paralysis. They quickly ran out of essentials like milk and bread. It was several days before they could be resupplied because delivery trucks could not negotiate the snowbound side streets. By Saturday, some shopkeepers were able to travel to the larger supermarkets on the main streets where they purchased some staples to restock their own shelves.

With the streets impassable, some building owners who heated with oil or coal began to worry about their supplies. There was no way that the fuel trucks could get to them until the streets were cleared. Fortunately, there were no reports of anyone in neighborhood without heat.

Looting was a problem in some parts of Chicago, but in the neighborhood only a few minor instances were reported. Two or three beer and soda trucks became mired in the side street snow and were abandoned by the drivers. Unknown parties then availed themselves of the trucks' contents.

Figure 61. Shoveling the walk during the 1967 storm. (Otto Kleiber, Chicago Tribune photo).

Figure 62. Cars and bus mired in the snow. (CBS 2 News).

Figure 63. Iowa Street east of Pulaski Rd. after the snow stopped. (Photo by Lucian Lutek).

Figure 64. Shoveling out Chicago Avenue near Central Park Ave. the evening after the storm. (Photo by Lucian Lutek)

CROSSTOWN EXPRESSWAY

The proposed Crosstown Expressway which would have been designated as Interstate 494 was a specter that hovered over the neighborhood for several years in the late 1960s and early 1970s. This expressway would have begun at the Dan Ryan Expressway near 75th St. and then would have proceeded northwestward toward Chicago's West Side where it generally follows the Belt Line Railway (near Cicero Ave.) northward to the Kennedy Expressway.

Chicago mayor Richard J. Daley and many transportation planners contended that the Crosstown would be an asset for West Side industrial concerns as it would provide better access to their facilities. Proponents also argued that the roadway provide motorists with a fast route between the Northwest and Southwest sides. A vast majority of neighborhood people opposed the Crosstown fearing not only the loss of their homes and little shops, but also the potential loss of community. Letters were written to politicians, meetings were held, and in the end, with the aid of Illinois governor Dan Walker who opposed the roadway, the project was shelved.

HAROLD GANGLER

Harold Gangler was the 31st Ward Republican committeeman. He maintained an office in the 4300 block of W. Division St. He was an alternate delegate to the 1972 Republican national Convention. When interviewed, several former residents of the neighborhood were familiar with his name, but could not place him or his activity. This is not surprising as the neighborhood and ward were solidly Democratic.

NEIGHBORHOOD STREET NAMES

Street names sometimes reflect the geography, history, or ethnicity of their region. Some of the neighborhood's streets actually do reflect such things. Most obvious is North Avenue named for being the city's northern boundary at the time of Chicago's incorporation in 1837. Division is another street name with a geographical connotation. Its name probably came from the fact that the street divides Goose Island in the North Branch of the Chicago River (Figure 65).

Several neighborhood streets are named for Chicago political and historical figures. Rice St. is named for John Blake Rice who was Chicago's mayor from 1865 to 1869. Several aldermen such as William L. Kamerling and Joseph Otto Kostner lent their names to a few of the area's streets. Builders, subdividers, and other real estate figures are also

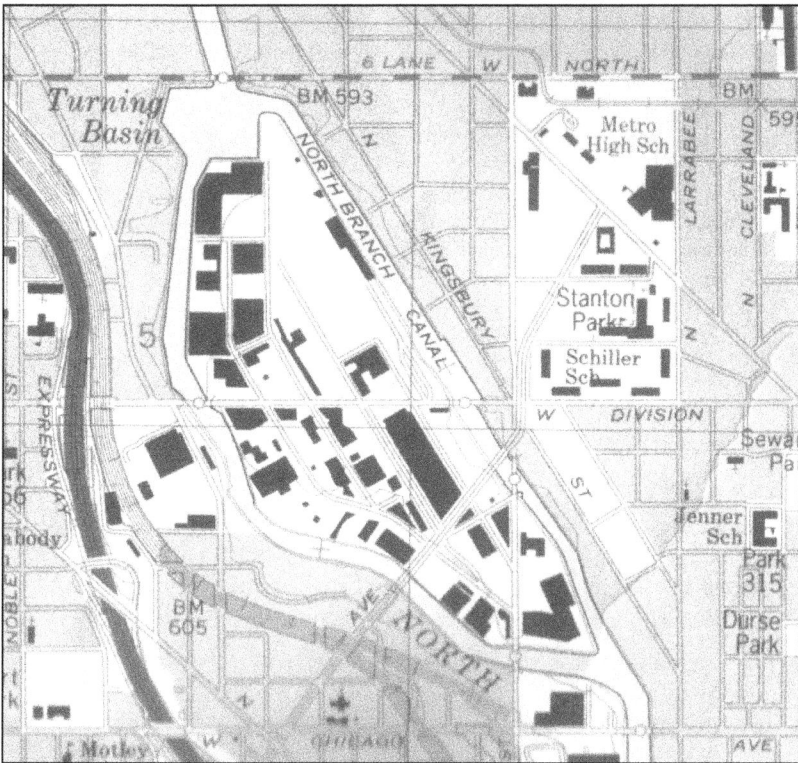

Figure 65. Division Street bisecting Goose Island.

79

represented on the street map. Pierce Avenue is named for Asael and M.J. Pierce whose land company in 1869 developed 80 acres in the vicinity of the street that bears their name. Thomas St. and Tripp Ave. may also have been named for real estate developers. Philo Carpenter, a pharmacist and real estate subdivider, named Augusta Blvd. for his daughter. There is some discrepancy regarding Hirsch St. Some sources believe it was named for Clemens Hirsch who was alderman of the 14th Ward along the North Branch of the Chicago River in the 1880s while others contend that it may have been named in honor of Reform rabbi Emil Gustav Hirsch who served as president of the Chicago Public Library Board in the 1880s.

A few streets in the neighborhood have an ethnic connection of sorts. Kolin Avenue was named for a small city in Bohemia (today Czech Republic) along the Elbe River. Karlov also has a Czech connection (Karlovy Vary) even though city records state the street was named for a town in Hungary (This is not a point of contention, however, as at the time the street was named, parts of Bohemia were in the Austro-Hungarian Empire). A similar situation arises with Kolmar Avenue which apparently named for a small town in Poland (Kolmar was the German name for Chodziec when the region near Poznan was controlled by Prussia). Ireland (County Kildare) is represented in the neighborhood by Kildare Ave. Although Kilbourn may sound Irish, that street was probably named after Kilbourn, a town near Wisconsin Dells.

The street at 4000 W. originally honored Peter Crawford who founded the settlement of Crawford which eventually became North Lawndale. In 1933 Chicago mayor Ed Kelly as a favor to his Polish-American supporters initiated the name change from Crawford Avenue to Pulaski Road. Business people along the street attempted to block the change claiming that it would create expense for them and confusion for their customers. It would take nineteen years, but in 1952 the Illinois Supreme Court finally settled the matter by ruling in favor of the name change. Still today, some Chicagoans on occasion call it Crawford Avenue.

NORTHWEST INCINERATOR

In the mid-1960s the City of Chicago proposed that a state-of-the-art garbage incinerator be built around 740 N. Kilbourn. This new facility was thought capable of reducing the city's volume of trash headed for landfills by 90%. It was promised to be safe and pollution-free, and would produce energy as a sideline. Environmentalists and neighborhood residents were skeptical and protests were filed. The city, however, prevailed and the Northwest Incinerator came on-line in 1971. The opening of this facility may have been one of several factors in the relocation decisions some neighborhood residents made during the decade.

At the time of its opening, the Northwest Incinerator was the world's largest municipal trash incinerator. It burned roughly 20% of the city's garbage. It ran for almost a quarter century, selling steam to the nearby Brach's Candy factory on and dumping lead and other pollutant emissions on the West Side neighborhoods. In 1993, a broad coalition of groups and individuals formed the Westside Alliance for a Safe and Toxic-free Environment to force the city to shut down the incinerator. In 1996, the incinerator was taken off-line and the facilities would serve as a garbage-transfer station.

Figure 66. Northwest Incinerator on Kilbourn south of Chicago Ave. (Courtesy of Marijke Rijsberman).

OUR LADY OF THE ANGELS SCHOOL FIRE

The school day at Our Lady of the Angels Catholic parochial elementary school was winding down on Monday December 1, 1958. Around 2:15 P.M. a fire that began in the basement was spreading and within a few minutes the conflagration would lead to the deaths of 92 children and 3 teaching nuns. Over one hundred children were injured in the fire and many more would bear mental and spiritual scars. The school at 3808 W. Iowa St. had an enrollment of 1635 students and it is estimated that somewhere between 1200 and 1400 children were in the school that fateful day.

The author was five years old and on the Division Street bus with his mother returning home from a downtown shopping trip around 3 P.M. that afternoon. His mother's remembrances of that day include hearing the sirens as the bus approached Kedzie Ave. (3200 W) and a few stops later learning of the fire from boarding passengers. The bus and other traffic may also have been diverted from Division Street for a few blocks so that emergency vehicles would not be impeded as they carried victims to nearby hospitals such as St. Ann's (4950 W. Thomas St.).

While the church and school were located just outside of the geographical confines of our neighborhood, Our Lady of the Angels (OLA) parish catchment area did include part of the eastern half of our neighborhood. Nine of the children who perished in the fire had lived west of Pulaski Road. Several of the victims were waked at the Kolssak Funeral Home on Division Street. For days there was a somber mood in the neighborhood as residents grieved and tried to comprehend the horror of that afternoon.

Tragic events like this one have long-term impacts, not only on the victims and their families, but also on the community-at-large. In the 1960s there was an exodus of Italian-American families from the OLA community and in some cases the tragedy no doubt was a personal factor. Jill Grannan a curator at the Chicago History Museum has stated "It seems as though people just couldn't get far enough away. I don't think the community ever really came back."(CathNews USA: 2008)). Demographic change in the OLA neighborhood east of Pulaski accelerated as the decade progressed in part due to unscrupulous realtors engaging in panic-peddling. In 1990, OLA and St. Francis of Assisi parishes merged. The rebuilt OLA school remained open until 1999. In 2009, the former OLA church building is home to a Baptist congregation and the rebuilt school building serves as the Galapagos charter school. The rectory is now the Our Lady of the Angels Mission with programs that assist the local poor and provide spiritual nourishment. A memorial to the fire victims is set on the front lawn.

Figure 67. O.L.A. School Fire (Chicago Daily News Photo).

EDWARD "BUTCH" PANCZKO

The Panczko brothers achieved legendary status in the annals of crime in Chicago. Born in the "Bad Lands" of Grand and Ogden in the 1920s and raised on W. Iowa Street in the Humboldt Park area, the three brothers, Edward "Butch", Joseph "Pops", and Paul "Peanuts" began their careers as young delinquents stealing capons and cheese and then graduated on to bigger heists. Throughout Chicago and beyond they pilfered just about anything-- Parker pens, jewelry, automobiles, and even a poodle. They heisted safes and were involved a Brinks job or two and their careers spanned almost a half of a century. They did on occasion work together, but most of the time they worked alone or with associates outside of the family. They worked hard at their craft, but in the long-term never amassed a great deal of money as they were caught often and spent a lot on legal services and bribing corrupt policemen. Chicago newspapermen gave the felonious brothers the title "Polish Robbin' Hoods". Over the course of their careers, Peanuts spent 26 years in prison and Pops served 20.

Edward "Butch" Panczko spent the last years of his life residing on Kedvale Avenue north of Thomas St. Arrested 77 times, Butch somehow managed to spend only 10 days in jail and had been fined a total of $113 in his career of thievery (Baumann and O'Brien: 1992). In January of 1956 he was involved in a botched burglary of the Mandel Brothers warehouse on the north bank of the Chicago River. Police had shot dead one of his accomplices and the State's Attorney, using a convoluted precedent, filed a murder change against Butch. A Criminal Court jury found him innocent. Butch Panczko passed away in 1978 at the age of 61. His funeral Mass was held at St. Philomena Catholic Church at 1921 N. Kedvale.

REZIN ORR SCHOOL

Rezin Orr School's history dates back to 1918 when it opened in rented quarters at Keeler and Augusta. The following year the school named after the railroad labor organizer was moved into a new building at 1040 N. Keeler Ave. The school's educational mission had varied over the years, but the building has always had an elementary school. At various times, the building has also served as a branch of Austin High School and a branch of Marshall High. Orr also offered vocational programs from 1935-1958. From 1958 to 1963, the building only housed an elementary school (For several years after their tragic fire, the Our Lady of the Angels Catholic School occupied the third floor). New building additions were constructed in the early 1960s and, from 1963 to 1973, Orr High School shared the expanded campus with the elementary school. In 2009, the building serves as Brian Piccolo Specialty School.

STREET SKEW AT NORTH AVENUE

Most of Chicago's streets adhere to a grid system oriented north-south and east-west with major thoroughfares located one mile apart. This is the legacy of the surveys performed in the Chicago area in the 1830s that followed the directives of the Northwest Ordinance of 1785. Much of the area west of the Appalachian Mountains was divided into townships of 36 square miles.

In the 1850s, Jefferson Township's southern boundary was North Avenue and the area south of that street that would eventually become the neighborhood of this study was part of unincorporated Cook County. In the parlance of the surveys, North Avenue would be considered a "town-line road". In many places in the Midwest, north-south roads "jog" at town-line roads. The townships were laid out based on Principal Meridians of longitude. Because of the curvature of the Earth (the meridians converge at the poles), with every few townships, there is a slight jog in the survey meridians to compensate. Along North Avenue from about Narragansett to the east edge of Humboldt Park the north-south streets are misaligned roughly 50-60 feet (Figure 68). For example, if one is driving north on Pulaski Road or Kildare Avenue, the street jogs to the right (east) about 60 feet on the other side of North Avenue.

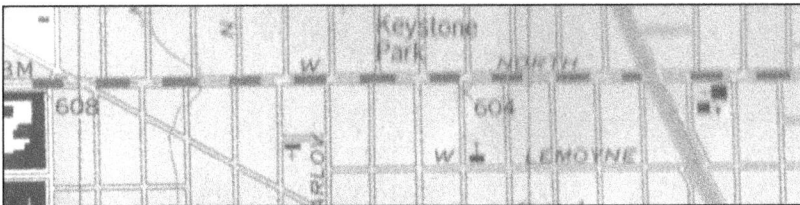

Figure 68. Street misalignment at North Avenue.

WEST SIDE RIOTS 1968

Rev. Martin Luther King Jr. was assassinated in Memphis, Tennessee on April 4, 1968. The gunshot that took his life violently reverberated through the streets of hundreds of American cities. On Chicago's West Side, rioting, arson, and looting were rampant for almost three days. Commercial streets like Madison and Roosevelt Road were hit particularly hard. Over 200 buildings were destroyed as snipers impeded the work of firemen. The city imposed a curfew on people under 21, liquor sales were stopped on the West Side, and police and National Guard troops guarded most intersections in the area. Eleven people, all African-Americans, were killed during the violent episode.

The devastation was occurring a little over a mile away from the neighborhood. Understandably, residents were apprehensive as the TV and radio news reported on the nearby riot. Rumors circulated of random violence in the immediate neighborhood, but these were all unsubstantiated.

People did notice an elevated police presence in the neighborhood and Jeeps carrying National Guard troops were spotted passing through. The sound of wailing sirens and the acrid smell of smoke punctuated the tension in the air. Some residents remember looking out of their second-story or attic windows at the smoke clouds and orange glow in the southern sky.

The enclave was physically spared, but the event did leave a mental mark on many residents. The neighborhood had been fortunate partly because of its isolation and partly because of protection provided by the authorities. But things were not going to be the same. The sense of security had been slightly eroded and a few residents began to consider relocation to the far Northwest Side or suburbia.

Figure 69. Aerial view of devastation of West Garfield Park/North Lawndale, April 5, 1968.   (Photo courtesy of Jay Ruby collection).

EPILOGUE:

THE NEIGHBORHOOD IN 2009

Neighborhoods are living organisms. They go through processes of birth, growth, evolution, morbidity, devolution, and in some cases, regeneration. Today the neighborhood is called K-Town by its residents who are primarily of Hispanic and African-American heritage. In the 1990s, the area was suffering with a number of modern urban pathologies, but indications are that the area is on the mend.

Many of institutions that were the neighborhood's cornerstones in the 1960s are gone, but others such as St. Francis of Assisi Church, Nobel School, and Jimmy's Red Hots remain to nourish the souls, minds, and bodies of the current population. There are still a few little corner groceries and neighborhood taverns and children still play at Augusta Park. Of course, there are new churches and new stores. Some things have changed and some things have remained, and some of the pillars on Kedvale Avenue still stand watch over the neighborhood.

Figure 70. Nobel School in 2009. (Photo by Mark Bowman).

REFERENCES

Books and articles

Anderson, Philip J. and Dag Blanck (eds.) 1992: Swedish-American Life in Chicago (University of Illinois Press).

Baumann, Ed and John O'Brien 1992: Polish Robbin' Hoods: The Inside Story of the Panczko Brothers, The World's Busiest Burglars (Bonus Books).

Bigott, Joseph C. 2001: From Cottage to Bungalow: Houses and the Working Class in Metropolitan Chicago, 1969-1929 (University of Chicago Press).

Bramadat, Paul and David Seljak 2008: Christianity and Ethnicity in Canada (University of Toronto Press).

Bruegmann, Robert 1993: Schaumburg, Oak Brook, Rosemont and the Recentering of the Chicago Metropolitan Area in John Zukowsky (ed.) Chicago Architecture and Design 1923-1993: Reconfiguration of an American Metropolis (Prestel Verlag).

Chicago Fact Book Consortium 1984: Local Community Fact Book, Chicago Metropolitan Area Based on the 1970 and 1980 Censuses. (Chicago Review Press).

Cutler, Irving 1982: Chicago: Metropolis of the Mid-Continent 3rd edition (Kendall/Hunt Publishing).

Goc, Micheal J. 1984: St. Francis of Assisi 1909-1984 (Taylor Publishing).

Grancki, Victoria 2004: Chicago's Polish Downtown (Arcadia Publishing).

Harris, Richard 1994: Chicago's Other Suburbs, *Geographical Review* Vol. 84:4

Hayner, Don and Tom McNamee 1988: Streetwise Chicago: A History of Chicago Street Names (Loyola University Press).

Hudson, John C. 2006: Chicago: Geography of the City and Its Region (University of Chicago Press).

Kantowicz, Edward R. 1995: Polish Chicago: Survival Through Solidarity, in Melvin G. Holli and Peter d' A. Jones (eds.) Ethnic Chicago: A Multicultural Portrait (William B. Eerdmans Publishing).

Keating, Ann Durkin (ed.) 2008: Chicago Neighborhoods and Suburbs: A Historical Guide (University of Chicago Press).

Kitagawa, Evelyn M. and Karl E. Tauber (eds.) 1963: Local Community Fact Book, Chicago Metropolitan Area 1960 (University of Chicago).

Koenig, Harry C. (ed.) 1980: A History of the Parishes of the Archdiocese of Chicago (Archdiocese of Chicago).

Lauderdale, Diane and Bert Kestenbaum 2000: Asian-American Ethnic Identification by Surname, *Population Research and Policy Review* Vol. 19.

Mayer, Harold M. and Richard C. Wade 1969: Chicago: Growth of a Metropolis (University of Chicago Press).

McGreevy, John T. 1996: Parish Boundaries: The Catholic Encounter With Race in the Twentieth Century Urban North (University of Chicago Press).

Monchow, Helen C. 1939: Seventy Years of Real Estate Subdividing in the Region of Chicago (Northwestern University).

Olson, Anita 1995: A Community Created: Chicago Swedes 1880-1950 in Melvin G. Holli and Peter d' A. Jones (eds.) Ethnic Chicago: A Multicultural Portrait (William B. Eerdmans Publishing).

Pacyga, Dominic A. and Charles Shanabruch 2001: The Chicago Bungalow Arcadia Publishing).

Reinemann, Martin W. 1960: The Pattern and Distribution of Manufacturing in the Chicago Area, *Economic Geography* 36.

Roucek, Joseph S. 1967: The Czechs and Slovaks in America (Lerner Publications)

Royko, Mike 1971: Boss: Richard J. Daley of Chicago (Penguin Books).

Samors, Neal 2006: Chicago in the Sixties: Remembering a Time of Change (Chicago's Books).

Samors, Neal and Michael Williams (eds.) 2003 : The Old Chicago Neighborhood: Remembering Life in the 1940s (Chicago's Neighborhoods, Inc.)

Seligman, Amanda J. 2005: Block By Block: Neighborhoods and Public Policy on Chicago's West Side (University of Chicago Press).

Streiker, Lowell 2005: The Old Neighborhood: Memories of a Chicago Childhood 1942-1952 (Lulu Press).

Tillman, Benjamin and Chad F. Emmett 1999: Spatial Succession of Sacred Space in Chicago, *Journal of Cultural Geography* Vol 18.

Turner, Jillian 1999: Slovak Immigrants in Illinois, *Illinois History* Vol. 53.

Websites

http://www.cathnewsusa.com/article.aspx?aeid=10501   Chicago's Our Lady of the Angels fire "changed everything"

http://www.chsmedia.org/househistory/nameChanges/start.pdf Chicago Historical Society

http://www.encyclopedia.chicagohistory.org Encyclopedia of Chicago History

http://www.gbgm-umc.org/nillconf/umrsep02.htm#092701   Northern Illinois Conference of the United Methodist Church Newsletter, September 2002.

http://olafire.com/   Our Lady of the Angels (OLA) School Fire, December 1, 1958

ABOUT THE AUTHOR

Anthony J. Dzik, Ph.D. is Professor of Geography at Shawnee State University in Portsmouth, Ohio. Originally from Chicago's West Side, Dzik was awarded the Ph.D. in Geography from Northwestern University. Before coming to Shawnee in 1988, he taught at Rosary College, Roosevelt University, and Chicago State University. His teaching and research interests are in medical geography, urban geography, regional geography of the Midwest and Great Plains, and popular culture. He is the author of ***Dodge Aspen and Plymouth Volare: An American Car Story*** (available from Sunfish Boulevard Publications/Lulu Press) and co-author (with J.W. Piety) of ***The Interpretation of Our Physical landscape: A Workbook***. He has published articles in such journals as *Geographia Medica, Bulletin of the Illinois Geographical Society, Public Health (London), Virginia Geographer, North Dakota Quarterly, West Virginia Medical Journal, Ohio Medicine, Ohio Journal of Science, Geographical Perspectives, South Dakota Journal of Medicine.* and *Transactions of the Illinois State Academy of Science*. He resides in southern Ohio with his wife, sons, and old Mopars.

www.ingramcontent.com/pod-product-compliance
Lightning Source LLC
Chambersburg PA
CBHW022029090426
42739CB00006BA/354